Effective Te

MW00711700

How to Sell over the Telephone

by

Allen Warfield and Al Brooks

Illustrations by Tanya Oliveira

Humor Books
Alexandria, VA

Humor Books
58 Donovan Place
Alexandria, VA 22306
(703) 360-5916

Quantity discounts available. Dealer inquiries welcome.

ISBN: 0-9633921-2-3

Contents

This book is dedicated to Jay Leno, Ed McMahon, Jack Benny, and George Burns.

This book is also dedicated to all the hard-working salesmen and telemarketers who are striving to improve their skills.

Introduction

It all began when Alexander Graham Bell first invented the telephone and said, "Watson, can you hear me?" . . . When Watson replied, "Yes", Alexander then tried to sell Watson a one-week vacation in the Bahamas.

Seriously, more and more firms are turning to telemarketing, or telephone sales to sell their products. Further, more and more salesman are contacting their existing and potential customers by phone first to cut down on the high cost and large amount of time spent on business travel. In addition, telephone selling has a much higher rate of sales than direct mail.

This book was written to make telephone sales smoother, more enjoyable, and more profitable. It can help increase your sales many times.

The Method

Perhaps the best method of <u>applying</u> the <u>basic principles</u> in this book is the method developed by Benjamin Franklin. The method can be used in selling, in business, or in flying a kite during a storm.
The method consists of:

1: Selecting the basic principles (preferably 10 to 15 principles).
2: Concentrate on 1 principle each week. The 2nd week, concentrate on the 2nd principle, the 3rd week concentrate on the 3rd principle, and so on.
3: At the end of 10 weeks, start the process all over again, concentrating on the first principle again for one week, and so on. Thus, during the course of a year, you'll go through the basic principles several times.

Below is a list of many of the <u>Basic Principles of Telemarketing</u>. You may wish to customize the list, adding or subtracting from it according to your own experience. But by following Franklin's method of concentrating on a single principle each week, you'll learn more and reap greater rewards.

1. Ask questions
2. Listen
3. Enthusiasm
4. Confidence
5. Know your product
6. Go the extra mile

7. Think and speak in terms of the customer's interests
8. Persistence
9. Sincerity
10. Set a goal and go for it. Plan, organize, prioritize.
11. Sell the time (interview time) before you sell the product
12. Help solve the customer's problems
12. Follow-up after the sale
13. Never argue or prove a customer wrong - rather find <u>solutions</u> for his objections
14. Talk in terms of <u>benefits</u> to the customer

Chapter 1: The Sales Pitch

Prepare a Written Sales Pitch or Outline in Advance

Keep a written sales pitch or outline out when you make your calls. Review the pitch frequently until it becomes familiar or almost automatic to you.
However, don't make it sound like you're delivering a memorized sales pitch. Try to sound "natural".
Natural salesmen, just like "natural" peanut butter, sell better.

Even if you're a salesman who's just calling on an existing customer, before you call, jot down a list or outline of the key points that you want to cover.
Review the list before the call, and keep the list handy during the call. This avoids having to keep calling the customer back several times, which is annoying, and it avoids embarrassment.

The usual sequence is:
- warm-up
- offer promotional gift
- short product pitch
- warm-up
- solidify - reaffirm product coming out to house
- product close - send out 1/2 case of product and give company information
- give details
- final close - have a great time at the golf course this weekend.

Break down your Sales Pitch
Into a Series of Questions

Take your present sales pitch, and convert it into a series of 5 to 10 questions that you <u>ask</u> the customer. The questions should be ordered so that the answers (should be "yeses"), and will lead to a logical decision to buy (or "try" your product without risk).

For example, one big accounting firm tries to get people to use their income tax preparation.

Salesman:	This is H. W. Blockhead and Associates.
Customer:	Yes.
Salesman:	Have you worked at all this year?
Customer:	Yes.
Salesman:	Have you PAID any taxes?
Customer:	Yes.
Salesman:	Would you like to get a refund?
Customer:	Yes.
Salesman:	Wouldn't you feel confident in getting a refund if a registered Blockhead prepared your taxes?
Customer:	Yes.

Ask Questions

The key is to ask <u>leading questions</u>. Thus, if you're selling hamburgers, you don't ask the customer what size shoes he wears. Likewise, if you're selling shoes, you don't ask if he would like an extra-greasy cheeseburger. Asking questions is far more effective than telling, isn't it? Lawyers, doctors, and other people who make a lot of money use this technique. Ask questions that will lead the buyer to an obvious conclusion - ultimately that he should buy your product.

Let's say you're selling memberships in a Singles Club for Messy and Sloppy People. Your first question:

Salesman:	Are you a slob?
Customer:	No.

(Hang up, and try again)

Salesman:	Are you a slob?
Customer:	Dah . . . I think so.
Salesman:	Do you have any hobbies?
Customer:	I usually take a chicken drumstick and bang it against a garbage can . . . I always wanted to be a drummer in a band.
Salesman:	So you're a chicken drummer . . . You'd fit right in; we have another guy who plays the guitar with a turkey leg. Then, we have a lady who plays the flute which she carved out of a carrot . . . And so on.

(Notice how the salesman is not just asking questions, he is trying to create interest in the product, in this case, other members of the singles group).

Ask Leading Questions

Lead the customer on.

Always keep customer answering "Yes". So, ask leading questions that encourage a positive (yes) answer.

And keep it flowing, so he can keep saying "Yes".

Never ask a question that he might give a negative answer to.

Here's a sample pitch from a salesman who sold garage door openers.

Salesman: Are you over 5 years old?
Customer: Yes.
Salesman: Do you have a house?
Customer: Yes.
Salesman: Do you have a car?
Customer: Yes.
Salesman: Do you have at least one hand?
Customer: Yes.
Salesman: Then, that's all you need to use one of our automatic garage door openers.

Opening Remarks. Introduce Yourself.

In your opening remarks, give your name and your company name. Also, give an opening statement that puts the prospective customer in a receptive frame of mind. For example, "I'm calling about a card you sent inquiring about our products." Or, "You were recommended to us by Johnny Appleseed of the Rotten Apple Applesauce Co." Or, "We read about your company in The Janitorial Times as having won the "Golden Mop" award."

First, You have to Get Their ATTENTION

If you don't have the prospects attention, it's very hard, if not impossible to sell him. There may be kids running around, the tv on, or if he's in the office, he may have the secretary, or the computer in the background. He may be looking through his mail, leafing through a magazine, or picking his nose. All these things are distracting (if not disgusting).

One method is to raise your VOICE. Another method is <u>silence</u>. For example, say, "Do I have your attention?" (Then be <u>silent</u> until he answers). Another method is to say something provocative, like "Oh, Mr. Simmons, in case you haven't noticed it, your house is on fire."

How to Begin Your Approach

First consider the customer's point of view: What does he or she really want?

If you <u>approach</u> a businessman about anything that will <u>cost him money</u>, he will immediately be turned off. He already has a hard time paying his rent, insurance, salaries, benefits, accountants, lawyers, etc. But if you <u>approach</u> him by <u>offering</u> a <u>solution to a problem</u> that he faces, he will begin to listen.

If you <u>approach</u> a homeowner about <u>buying a new appliance</u> or <u>gadget</u> for their home, he or she will probably be turned off. But if you approach the housewife or her husband by offering a way to <u>save them money</u>, <u>reduce wasted food</u>, <u>save energy</u>, <u>cut down on their utility bills</u>, or <u>reduce the cost</u> of their grocery bills, their ears will perk up - and you will have their attention.

Be Specific

Use specific quantities and amounts wherever possible. For example, don't say: It could save you a lot of money. (How much is "a lot"?) It's better to say, It could save you $10,000.

One salesman sold women's cosmetics. Sales were okay. Then, one day a customer called and thanked him for the cosmetics, which helped her get a date with a younger man. Naturally, he asked - How much younger? It turns out he was 10 years younger. (She was 102, and he was 92). Anyway, he worked it into his sales pitch, "Our cosmetics could make you look 10 years younger." . . . Naturally, sales soared.

Make it Believable

Don't be so strong in your claims that nobody will believe it. For example, one salesman sold vitamins. His opening was, "Our vitamins will help make you healthier, bigger, and stronger. In less than a year, you'll grow to be 10 feet tall."

Customize your Pitch to the Audience

If he's a high roller, maybe he's interested in the stock market, finance, or investments. If he's a couch potato, maybe he's interested in what happened on Gilligan's Island, or maybe, he's a fan of Leave it to Beaver. Offer to get him a piece of toilet paper with Wally's signature on it.

Maybe he's an avid sports fan. If he's from Washington, say you can get him a Washington Redskins tee-shirt, an autographed football, or a small piece of one of the fullback's broken bones. If he's from Chicago, offer him a Michael Jordan tee-shirt, or if he's a really good customer, offer him one of Michael Jordan's used shoelaces.

Ask Questions. Questions help you to find out what a customer's needs and problems are. For example, a customer states that a certain man is a golfer. The salesman asks, "How do you know?" The customer replies, "He has a golfer's nose, you know, it hooks to the left"...Knowing the man is a golfer (at least his nose is a golfer) can lead to sales.

Vary Your Pitch by Geographic Area

Vary your pitch according to where you are calling. You can lengthen or shorten your conversation depending on where you are calling. People tend to talk longer in rural areas than urban areas. People also tend to talk longer in the South and Southwest than the North and East. The West Coast and Midwest are intermediate length, longer than the East, but not as long as The South.

Verbal Commands

Strong verbal commands, though subliminal, make the customer more receptive to buying your product. It's sort of like "hypnosis". Before he comes out of the spell, he's already bought your product. Is your voice and sales pitch "hypnotic", or does it sound like a hippo?

Thus, you implant a subconscious thought or command in your customer's mind. Use statements like:

That makes sense to you, Joe?

Wouldn't it be better to try Product A, than continue using your old half-good product?

A rock rolls downhill, doesn't it, Joe?

That makes sense to you, Joe?

Names and Faces

Whenever possible, state the person's name, and work it into the conversation. Dale Carnegie said, "A man's name is to him the sweetest and most important sound in the English language."

One salesman was calling on a customer, Mr. and Mrs. Irving Camelwart, about a new product: a combination toaster and vacuum cleaner.

Salesman: (The phone rings) Hello, Mrs. Camelwart?

Customer: Yes.

Salesman: Mrs. Camelwart, we're offering a new product. Did you ever want to cook some toast while you were vacuuming the carpet?

Customer: Not that I remember.

Salesman: Well, Mrs. Camelwart, . . . Now you can . . . Further, the device saves you money. All that heat generated when you are vacuuming up a dusty carpet won't be wasted - it can cook toast. What's more, Mrs. Camelwart . . . When you burn toast, till it's dark brown or black, it's not wasted, you can use the burned toast as a dust filter for the vacuum cleaner.

Use Word Pictures

When you speak, the customer is like a blind man - he can't see what you are talking about. (So offer him a white cane) . . . Better yet, use your words to paint vivid pictures of what you are talking about. Since the customer is on the telephone, he can't actually see your product (If he could see it, he wouldn't buy it). Hence, you need to create pictures in your customer's mind that will entice him to buy.

For example, let's say, you're selling lard. Tell your customer: We only sell grade A lard; it's white like whale blubber. It's soft and smooth like lipstick.

16

In fact, one famous Cosmetic company uses our lard in its lipstick . . . And we get our lard only from contented pigs . . . pigs that are content to lay in a pile of mud all day.

Should you use Jokes or Humor in Selling?

That's like asking: Is a bear Catholic, or does the Pope shit in the woods? Humor "breaks the ice". It also prevents boredom. A joke livens up the presentation. It adds spice to meat, it adds flavor to Spam. (What the heck is Spam anyway?) If you can get your customer to laugh, he will probably like you, and is more likely to buy something from you.

Find out his "hot button"

In the warm-up, determine the customer's likes and dislikes away from the office: Does he like to fish, hunt, golf, or play tennis in his spare time. Find out his "hot button".

Let's say his hot button is golf . . . Then say, "It's our 25th Anniversary and we're running a promotion - we got a whole case of Titalist golf balls." Then, get his home address. Say: "We used to send them to the plant, but the gift gets lost at loading dock, or a clerk picks it up and decides to keep the golf balls. So, what I'm going to do is insure them by UPS and send the golf balls directly to the house to make sure you personally get it . . . That makes sense to you, Joe?"

By sending the golf balls directly to the house, you're getting a commitment: that he has to listen to what you're selling. Also, indirectly, by accepting a

Know your product. In this case,
your product can vacuum the carpet and
make toast at the same time.

gift, he realizes that there's a product that he has to buy along with it.

Choices

Limit the number of choices to just a few. If you offer 20 or 30 choices, the customer will probably never make up his mind. For example, if you are selling hair-color products, don't offer 50 different colors, say, "What color would you like: natural black, autumn blond, or baby-shit brown?"

Giving the customer a choice is a good way to "close" the sale. For example, you can say, "Would you like to pay by check or credit card?" "Would you like it delivered Thursday or Friday?"

Always give a customer a choice between "yes" and "yes". For example, "Would you like to take it now or would you like us to deliver it in 3 weeks?" Or, "Would you like the green one or the red one?" "Would you like the one-liter bottle or the 6-pack?"

One salesman was selling house slippers made out of crabgrass. He would offer a choice, "Would you like our regular slippers or our extra-crabby crabgrass slippers?"

Sample Sales Pitch with Warm-up

Here is a sample sales pitch that is used by a successful company.

1. Hello, I'm calling in response to the card you sent in for our custom line of schmidgets. I appreciate your interest.

2. (Warm-up. Find the customer's hot spot.) Joe, what do you like to do in your spare time?

3. Hey Joe, I'm going to send you that dogbone that was on the card. It's a real beauty. (Romance the dogbone, Describe it).

4. Joe, I used to send these dogbones right to the plant, but they always end up in the wrong hands. So now, I send them right to the home, UPS insured. Joe, what's your home address?

5. Fine Joe, give me a week to 10 days for the bones to arrive in the mail . . . and do me a favor, promise me you'll get a bite out of them (and you won't bury them).

6. Hey Joe, about the product. These are Industrial Strength schmidgets.
   . . . . They resist rust.
   . . . . . They have low friction and wear.
   . . . . And they don't stink up your plant.

7. We normally package schmidgets in cases of 12 dozen at $4.90 per dozen. But what I'm going to do is break that down for you and get out a 1/2 case of 6 dozen schmidges and maintain the bulk rate. In other words, you'll get schmidges for the same price as schmidgets.

8. Oh, by the way, we have some things left over from our cowpie Promotion, and let me ask you something . . . . We have some real nice cowpies left over. You know the ones with . . . .. (Describe it).

9. Let me ask you, Joe, would you get more use out of these real nice cowpies, or would you rather stick with the dogbone?

10. Great, Joe, let me check that home address.

11. Like I said, give me about 2 weeks on the bones, and do me a favor, give me about 3 or 4 weeks on the 1/2 box of the schmidges, and when I call you back in 5 or 6 weeks, I want you to tell me that you got some use out of this.

12. Joe, grab a pencil, and I'll give you my company information.

13. Hey, Joe, I appreciate the business, but more than that, it's been great talking to you. I'll be talking to you again in 5 or 6 weeks. Hey, Joe, I almost forgot, I'll need an order number on this. What is your next Purchase Order Number?

14. Thanks, Joe, ... (SHORT WARM UP, Then Say Good-Bye).

Chapter 2: The Customer

Get to Know Your Customer

One of the most important things in telemarketing is to get to know your customer. I remember when I first met a great salesman, Bill "Bananabrain" Pilgrim. Bananabrain had a knack with people. He could virtually "peel" away a person's exterior, and talk to the real person underneath, which was often not much better than the outer person.

Know your Customer

The more you know about your customer, the better your chances of solving his particular set of problems, and the better the chance of getting a sale. Each week, professional football coaches and their players spend hours watching and analyzing the team they will meet the following Sunday. How much time do you spend each week studying and analyzing your customer and <u>his</u> needs?

Talk on the Same Level

Always talk on the same level as your customer. Never make it like you're an authority, or you're above him. He's the <u>authority</u>. Listen to him, ask and listen for his advice - ask his <u>needs</u>. So, never talk down to a customer. Always talk on an even level. Make him your friend. Be interested in what <u>he has to say</u>, not just what you have to say.

So, never put yourself above the customer, always put yourself on the same level. Be courteous and sincere.

Speak the Customer's Language

What the customer doesn't understand, he won't buy. More than that, by speaking the customer's language (add "Y'all" for southern calls, or "You's guys" up North), he'll feel more at home.

One salesman, had a hard time with some of the slow talkers living in the hills. The one friend suggested, "If you want to relate to the hill people, you've got to talk with marbles in your mouth." So Stan tried it. It was uncomfortable at first, . . . but after a while he got used to it. Soon, his sales to the hill people exceeded his sales to people living on flat land or in igloos.

Talk in terms of the Customer's Interest

According to Dale Carnegie, "There is only one way under heaven to get anybody to do anything, and that is by making the other person <u>want</u> to do it." . . . Thus, the key is to: **find out what the other person wants, then help him find the best way to get it . . .**

However, in order to find out what the other person wants, you have to ask a few questions, and do <u>a lot of listening</u>. Then, once you've found out what his true <u>interests</u> or wants are, find a way to help him get what he wants (especially if it's by buying one of your products). But even if it's not by actually buying your products, by listening and helping him - maybe by giving him a connection - leading him to another person he should see - he will be more receptive and thankful for - and more likely to buy what you are selling.

For example, one customer desires that his son become a basketball star. The salesman listened as the man described how his son had scored 22 points in one game earlier that year . . . Then, the salesman suggested the name of a summer basketball camp (with a great coach) that the boy might attend. He even offered to check with a relative who knew more about it. The result: the customer "bought" the basketball camp idea, and he also bought the salesman's product: imitation cotton balls. (Of course, he explained how the cotton balls could protect the boy's valuable hearing, so he could hear the coach yelling from the sidelines, "Shoot, you idiot.")

<u>Listen carefully</u> for a customer's hobbies and interests. You may even ask, do you play golf? or tennis? or fish? Did you see last Sunday's football, or basketball, or baseball game? (Note whether or not the customer is enthusiastic about, doesn't care, or didn't even watch it).

Think in Terms of the Customer

Think in terms of your customer. What are you giving to him that will be of <u>interest</u> to <u>him</u>. The customer doesn't care what's important to you; he cares about what's important to himself. Once you can think like your customer thinks, then you can keep 2 steps ahead of him. You can understand his needs, and his fears. Then, you can help satisfy his needs, and allay his fears.

Let's say, you're selling rotten bananas . . . Grade A rotten bananas . . . Think of your customer.

Talk in terms of the customer's interests. Here, a customer is having an outdoor cook-out. You can practically smell the food burning.

Who would want rotten bananas? Maybe an old lady with no teeth . . . So you call Nursing Homes. They're delighted to buy bananas for 5 cents/lb. They say, "most old people won't even notice - especially when we mix the bananas with milk and pudding." Who else would want it? Women who bake. There's a proverb, "The rottener the banana, the better the banana cream pie."

Do your Customer a Favor

Ask how about ordering a case. If he says, I can't order a case, say I'll tell you what, I'll do you a favor, and break a case, or break a drum for you. How about 1/2 a case, you can handle that." (If not, try a quarter case).

Then, hit his "hot button", having a promotion (tie into hobbies), tell him that we'll send out those dozen golf balls to your home, you should have them in a week to 10 days. A lot of times plants frown upon employees receiving personal gifts, so send it out to his house.

Find out what the Customer's Needs Are

Seek to understand what your customer needs to buy, rather than what you want him to have. Let's say you're selling toothpicks, and you want the customer to buy your toothpicks, but what your customer really needs is a brain transplant. So, sell him a new brain.

Another approach is to: 1st - Find out the customer's needs. 2nd - Then, explain how your product can satisfy those needs.

Find out what the Customer's Problems Are

How?
1. By asking: Are you having any difficulties in the plant? Or, are you having any problems with your present product?

2. By listening: Don't tell the customer what his problem is; let him tell you what his problem is.

Complaints and Criticism

Listen to the customer. Especially listen to any complaints or criticisms that he has about either your product or your competitor's product. Write down the complaints, for it is these complaints that help you grow. Finding a way to satisfy the complaints, can come from discussions with the Corporate President, the Chief Engineer, or by talking with one of the janitors.

For example, one salesman sold Kangaroo pouches. And his pouches were autographed by Captain Kangaroo himself. One of the customers complained that the pouches were hopping on his desk . . . The salesman suggested he could stop the hopping by hitting the pouches over the head with a pet rock.

Treat the Customer like a Friend

Whenever possible, treat the customer like he's a friend. If he feels like you're a friend, he's more likely to trust you, and more likely to buy. So what is a friend? According to a proverb that I read on the back of a tea bag . . .

"A friend is someone who
Understands your past,
Believes in your future,
And accepts you just the way you are."

Here's an example:

Salesman:	Hello, this is Mr. Fletcher of the Fillmore Meat Co., Is Mr. Wilson home?
Customer:	Yes, this is Barnyard Wilson.
Salesman:	May I call you Barnyard? . . . Barnyard, that's an unusual name. How did you get it?
Customer:	My friends used to call me Barnyard because I smelled like one.
Salesman:	What do you do?
Customer:	I was really ugly, so for the past 10 years, I got a job as a scarecrow . . . Then one day, I got hit in the face by one of those corn-picking machines . . . My face really got bashed up, so I've been unemployed.
Salesman:	If your face is really bashed up, you should apply for a job as a hockey player.

This is an example of a salesman offering some "friendly" advice.

Recognition and Appreciation

Give <u>appropriate recognition,</u> and <u>appreciation,</u> and <u>praise</u> to a customer (or a fellow employee).
Thanks for your business.
That was a great tennis match you played.

Congratulations on winning the Layz Potato Chip Competition. I heard you ate 400 bags. That's quite an achievement—eating 400 lbs. of potato chips in one day . . . I heard somebody ate 408 bags, but he was disqualified because he exploded.

Compliments and Praise

The highest compliment you can pay a man is: <u>listening to him</u>. (See other section on listening). When you give praise, remember the quote of a great poet, what's his name, "The difference between blarney and baloney . . . Baloney is so thick you can cut it with a knife . . . Blarney is so thin you just love it." So when you give praise or compliments, don't make it so thick, that it's obviously baloney.

Try to be honest . . . for example, you might say the person sounds like someone famous, such as "You sound like Robert Redford, or Jack Nicholson, or Larry in The Three Stooges right after Moe pulled some of Larry's hair out." Also, subtle compliments are easier to give, such as "You sound thin" (which women like). A subtler way of saying it might be "You sound like a toothpick." . . .

Chapter 3: Listen

Silence

Ben Franklin considered "silence" one of the basic tenements of success. Ben's proverb was: "Silence: talk little, listen much." Ask simple questions. And let the customer do most of the talking.

The basic technique is to: First, find out what the customer is <u>interested</u> in. Then, direct the conversation in that area by asking questions that the customer will <u>enjoy</u> answering. Then, <u>listen</u>. Nothing is more flattering or more effective in selling than just listening.

For example, one salesman sold flakes (cereal flakes, not flaky people) . . . He called one customer, who he found out was a magician. He directed the questions in that area, "What's your favorite trick?" The magician replied, "Sawing Salesmen in half." . . . He then asked, "How do you do it?" . . . This, of course, led to a demonstration . . . The outcome - the salesman got half an order.

Be a Good Listener

The most important quality of a salesman is not to be a good talker, but to be a <u>good listener</u>. Too many salesman have such a good pitch memorized, that they don't give the customer a chance to get a word in edgewise. By listening to the customer, the customer will gain confidence in you. It's good to share your ideas, but encourage the customer to share his ideas too.

Also, by being a good listener, it will help you to pick up or detect his "hot buttons" or "green (buying) lights".

Listen. Sales are made not by talking but by listening. You should be "all ears" (like the man above).

Chit Chat

Successful salesman and telemarketers can relax and chat with a customer about the customer's business and interests that are not related to what the salesman is selling. The ability to chat in a friendly manner shows the customer you're interested in him, and leads to sales later in the conversation.

For example, one telemarketer who sold raincoats, called on a Mrs. M from Iowa. Mrs. M happened to have a bad foot fungus. The telemarketer listened to the lady describe her fungus feet. The telemarketer even offered advice on baking her feet in the oven, using footwarmers, and subscribing to "Fungus World" magazine. The result: The customer ordered 6 raincoats (which kept her feet dry & fungus free).

Never Argue

Remember, "Never argue with a customer." As Ben Franklin said, "The best way to win an argument is to avoid it." When you argue with a customer - he only becomes more angry, and almost certainly won't buy, whether or not you "prove" him wrong. The idea in telemarketing is not to win arguments, but to win sales. So avoid arguments at all costs, and whenever possible, find something to <u>agree</u> with in what the customer says.

For example, one salesman sold "screw-up" insurance . . . He told potential customers: "It's insurance for students who screw up on their final exams and can't get in college." One customer replied, "But I thought most screw-ups went to community college." The salesman could have argued, citing that he knew some screw-ups that became US Senators . . . Instead, he said, "Yes, Mr. Bottlecap, it's true, most community colleges accept almost anyone, even if they're in a mental coma. But think of all his friends and relatives who subtly insult him under their breath. Our insurance pays you for each insult."

One of the big restaurant chains (who sold over 25 billion hamburgers) has the motto, "The customer is always right." If necessary, swallow your pride, but never argue, get defensive, or antagonize the customer. When you argue with, you put the customer on the defensive - you put him on the opposing team. Likewise, when you act defensive, you're acting like you're on the opposing team. Whereas, you really want to act like you're on the <u>same team</u>. And when you win, you <u>both win</u> (you're helping him win).

For example, one salesman was selling special bird seed: if you plant it, it grows birds. One customer complained that when he planted the birdseed, a bird grew all right, but it had the brains of a cucumber. What's worse, this bird with a cucumber brain was running for public office.

At first, the salesman starting arguing that his birdseed was good, and everyone he knew had raised birdbrains. The customer argued that he knew a cucumberbrain when he saw one, and that he was very worried that the cucumberbrain might get elected instead of the usual birdbrain.

Once the salesman calmed down, he realized that the customer had probably planted the bird seed in an old cucumber patch. He suggested bribing the cucumber with some lettuce or having an affair with a tomato. Then, once the cucumber, lettuce, and tomato were together, he could make a salad. (Hence, it's extremely difficult to sell when you argue with the customer).

Empathy

In addition to listening, you need to have empathy. Sympathy is feeling sad when the other person feels sad. It is feeling the same feelings as he is. As Barry Manilow sings, "I'm sad when you're sad; I'm glad when you're glad." This may be good for love, but it's terrible if you're trying to eat a pizza . . . Better than sympathy is to have empathy. Empathy is understanding how the other person feels, without actually feeling bad yourself. Empathy allows you to "understand" your customer's problems, then help him find a solution. By being objective, you can better help the customer find a solution. If you're too closely involved, like a brother or a sister, mother or father, it's hard to be objective, and often hard to offer the best solution.

For example, one salesman is selling hairspray that holds your hair so strong that you can put a dozen bricks on your head.

Salesman:	How are you today Ma'am?
Customer:	Terrible. My cat has fleas.
Salesman:	How many?
Customer:	500 billion.
Salesman:	That's too bad . . . Hmm, maybe we can help?
Customer:	Really?
Salesman:	Yep. You can spray your cat with our Superhold hairspray. It is so gooey and sticky that the fleas will be stuck together. Our hairspray is really very much like fly paper. Insects stick to it and can't get away. One woman had over 100 flies stuck to her head.

34

Never argue with a customer. When you argue, you lose sales. When you get into a heated argument, smoke will come out of your ears.

Chapter 4: The Product

Know the Product

The best telemarketers know their products, and their customer. They can get the customer to understand the product, like the product, and want the product. They can get the customer to keep coming back for more product. Repeat customers are the foundation of every successful business.

A good example is drug dealers who rely on dope addicts to keep coming back. Another example is bars that rely on alcoholics and drunks.

The more you know about your product, the more <u>enthusiastic</u> about it you can get, the more <u>benefits</u> you can explain to your customers, the more <u>angles</u> you can use to sell it. Thus, one benefit may sell one customer, but it may be another benefit that sells another customer. The more you know your product, the more <u>benefits</u> you will know, the more customers you can sell.

One salesman sold hammers - all different sizes and types of hammers. One day, he called a customer, but all the customer did was complain about his lumpy oatmeal . . . So, the salesman talked to his boss and they decided to come out with a hammer specially designed to break up the lumps in a bowl of oatmeal. Within 6 months, "lumpy oatmeal hammers" were his biggest seller. His enthusiasm grew, for what is more satisfying than taking a hammer and smashing the lumps in oatmeal. Further, it led to added sales - mostly bibs and aprons - to protect customer's clothing against flying pieces of oatmeal due to vigorous hammering.

Know your Competition

Knowing your competition helps you overcome objections, and focus on the advantages of your product over the competition. Never directly knock the competition. For example, if you are selling paint, don't say your competitor's paint stinks, say "your paint covers the wall in two coats compared to 17 coats for your competitor."

Know your competitor's strengths - for example, low price. Also, know your product's strengths, especially where it is better than the competition. You might say, "Yeah, XYZ paint is low cost. In fact, a gallon of their paint is nearly the same price as a gallon of water - what a coincidence. However, quality paint costs a little more, but it lasts a lot longer.

Talk in Terms of Benefits

Whenever you are talking about your product, don't talk in terms of features, talk in terms of <u>benefits</u> to your customer. For example, let's say you're selling cigars. Don't say: Our cigars are 10 inches longer, and made with fine Columbian tobacco. Say our cigars come with a special holder for smokers that are toothless . . . Further, the cigars smoke smooth and light; you'll feel like you haven't got a brain in your head.

Know your Product: Features and Benefits

This includes <u>limitations</u> of the product. Most importantly, make a list of all the features of the product, preferably in one column on a sheet of paper.

Then in another column, for each feature, list the corresponding benefit (to the customer). Then, when talking to a customer: <u>talk in terms of benefits</u>, not features.

For example, Let's say the product is "shoes".

Feature	Benefit
made of leather	long wear, comfortable
hand-sewn	won't come apart, long-lasting, good value
foam heel	comfortable, especially for long walks
pointed toe	can kill cockroaches in the corner

Selling is easier if you think in terms of how it will <u>benefit</u> the customer. Nobody buys anything if there's not a benefit.

State your Biggest Benefit First

If you don't state the biggest or most important benefit up front, many listeners may tune you out. For example, "How would you like to save $5,000 a year?" Immediately, the listener's ears will perk up. Your first few statements, if you want to get their attention, should be like <u>NEWSPAPER HEADLINES</u>. Read all about it. "The President Marches on Capitol Hill and Steps on a Piece of Bubblegum."

What's New?

Besides explaining the benefits to your customer, bring something new or different. Have you got a new or improved product? People are usually interested in what's new (especially if you're excited about it). It may be a new product, or a new vacation deal. Whatever you're selling - what's new or different about it?

Quality

The quality of your products should always equal, or preferably surpass that of your competitors. Let's say you are selling chicken beaks, and your customers are chickens or people who look like chickens. If your competitor's chicken beaks can cluck 10 times per minute, your chicken beaks must be at least 1 cluck better.

Value

You've got to give value. People won't buy something if they think they're getting rooked, or they're overpaying. Value doesn't mean cheap. It means they're getting something of value for their money. Peanuts may be cheap, but 100% dry-roasted peanuts may be something of value, especially if the jar of peanuts was autographed by Jimmy Carter.

Value is an individual thing. What's valuable to one person may have little or no value to another. A big benefit of your product to one customer may not be a benefit at all to another. Hence, that's why it pays to know as much about your customer as possible (usually by "listening" to him).

For example, one telemarketer sold "Big Mama Pimple Cream". It was especially designed for those "Big Mama pimples". Her primary customers were teenagers. Obviously, "Big Mama Pimple Cream" was far more valuable to a teenage girl with a pimple on the end of her nose, especially before a date, than it would be to a bum, a wino, or a computer geek.

Talk in Terms of Value

Whatever the price of the item you are selling, talk in terms of the "value", especially to the customer. If you're selling earrings, maybe they're 24-karat gold, or 18-karat gold filled, or spray painted with something that looks like gold. If you're selling a vacation cruise, maybe it's on a "luxury liner", and you get 7 days for the price of 5 days, or if the ship sinks after 3 days, you get a refund on the unused portion.

Another way to express value is if the product lasts longer, or costs less in maintenance or repairs. It might have a higher "initial price", but over the lifetime of the product, the total cost to the customer will be less. Thus, there are many ways to show value to a customer.

For example, one salesman sold an elite line of couches. A customer asked, "I'd like something the color of Budweiser . . . so when I spill some, you won't notice the spots . . . " The salesman asked, "Regular or Budd-light?" . . . The customer replied, "Regular. And I'd like a couch that isn't too fuzzy . . . Our present couch, after you sit on it, a bunch of fuzz sticks to your pants." The salesman remarked, "Okay, Budd-Regular,

No-Fuzz . . . " The salesman is giving the customer the value he wants: A Budd-Regular couch with No-Fuzz.

Talk in Terms of Solving Problems

Don't sell products; sell solutions. For example, if your product is toilet bowl cleaner, don't say to your customer: "How would you like some toilet bowl cleaner?" Don't sell products. Sell solutions. In other words, sell your customer a solution to getting rid of that awful smell.

Remember, don't sell products, sell <u>solutions to problems</u>. People will buy solutions to their "perceived" problems. Thus, the key is to show the customer what his or her problem is and how your company's products or services can solve it. For example, let's say you're selling soap. You might say, "Do people hold their noses when they talk to you?" . . . "Do people compare you to a rotten egg?" . . . Our soap, "Head and Armpits" can solve your problems. Soon, people will no longer flee from you, they'll cling to you, so you'll have to beat'em off with a rake.

Break it Down to a Small Amount

Whatever your product or service, if it costs a little more than your competitors, break down the difference, per month, or preferably per day. For example, if your product is $110, and your competitor's is $100, (and of course yours is better in some way), then your product is $10 more. But spread the $10 over the life of the product. Let's say the product will last 2 years, then that's only $5/year, or only 1 1/2 cents per day. Isn't it worth 1 1/2 cents a day more to have a cleaner house (if you're selling vacuum cleaners). Or let's say you're selling toaster ovens with an automatic dinger that "dings" when the toast is done. Isn't it worth 1 1/2 cents a day so your whole house doesn't smell like burnt toast, and you don't have to listen to your husband yelling at you, "Can't you cook a piece of lousy toast."

Imagination and the Many Forms of your Product

Top-notch basketball players imagine themselves putting the ball through the hoop. Even when they are injured, they "practice" by imagining themselves shooting baskets, and scoring. Hence, it pays to imagine yourself making a sale . . . You can also use your imagination and creativity to get new leads and more sales . . . Imagine the many forms of your product . . . Then, imagine, who might use it in each of the different forms. One salesman sold bellybutton lint . . . Lint sales were a little slow for the day. Then, he began to imagine the many forms that bellybutton lint could take . . . First, a fuzzy ball, then a clump, then it could be rolled up into thread like yarn, and then the yarn could be knitted into sweaters . . . That was the idea that set him off. He called several yarn and sweater manufacturers, and offered them a low-cost, but strong source of yarn. The result: he got some very big sales. And as a bonus, the manufacturer gave his wife a beautiful sweater made out of bellybutton lint.

Chapter 5: Integrity, Trust, and Service

Integrity and Trust

There's a proverb, "In God We Trust; all others pay cash." . . . Perhaps the most important thing in telemarketing, or selling almost anything, is to gain the trust of the customer. If the customer likes you and trusts you, he will probably buy. If he doesn't trust you; he probably won't buy. A good example of loss of trust is a man by the name of "Tricky Dick". It was a loss of trust that cost Tricky Dick the Presidency. Trust, sincerity, and integrity should come from within, and not be like a burp after a big meal.

In many cases, a customer may see the value of the product, and can afford the price, but won't buy because he <u>fears</u> he may be being conned into something. If the customer does not <u>trust</u> the salesman, or believe in his integrity, he won't buy. However, if he does trust the salesman's integrity, in most cases, he will buy the product.

Don't promise what you or your product can't perform. And whatever you promise, make sure to deliver. A good example is the growth of Dominos pizza - delivery in 30 minutes or $3 off. Or Federal Express - "Guaranteed Overnight Delivery" . . .

Another example is "Sally's Spider Shop". Sally sold spiders (and webs) to government, universities, and industry. If a spider broke a leg, she'd step on it, rather than sell it. Sally's motto was, "We won't sell defective spiders - all our spiders can crawl and climb walls." That's a big promise. It led to a big order from Arnie's Deli, who was trying to get rid of its 50 million flies.

Sincerity. People buy from people they can trust. Would you buy a used car from Sadam Husein? No, why not? Just because the car contains poison gas and you have to use a gas mask to drive it.

Sincerity

Inherently, a lot of people don't trust salesmen. One way of gaining someone's trust is by being sincere. Franklin considered "sincerity" one of his 13 articles of faith upon which he based his life. Franklin wrote, "Sincerity: Use no harmful deceit, think justly, and if you speak, speak accordingly."

One salesman sold vitamins, all types of vitamins. But after calling and talking to many people, he realized that some vitamins were needed by more people than others. For example, one vitamin was especially suited for people with clogged up brains . . . So, instead of always telling everybody about all the vitamins, whenever he came upon a person who was groping for words, he said, "Does your brain need unclogging?" He sold more vitamins that way . . . By being direct, he wasted less time, helped more people, and sold more.

Be sincere. Never give the impression that you're cheating or pressuring your customer. Kill him with kindness and sincerity.

Customers resent misleading salesman. So early in your pitch, you will need to tell the customer: Who you are? Whom you represent? The nature of the call (what you are selling). For example, one salesman might begin by saying, "I'm Paul Cactushead from the Grateful Granite Company . . . We're having a special right now - buy one tombstone, get one free."

Friends

Whenever possible, whether or not you make a sale, at least make a friend. That person, some time in the future, may refer you to a relative, or may

himself place an order. Or he may give you <u>advice</u>
that may help you get other orders with other
customers.

When you treat a <u>customer</u> as a <u>friend</u>, you
care about them, you take care of their needs. Let's
see how 2 salesmen handle difficult customers:

Customer: I'm sorry, but I'm not interested in
         ordering now.
Salesman 1: May a bird of paradise leave droppings
         on your car.
Salesman 2: I'm sorry that you can't order just now,
         but maybe we can send you a couple
         samples and our catalog.
         By the way, if you're ever in Houston,
         . . .

Always end on a <u>positive note</u>. Remember, the biggest
sales, and the biggest customers are rarely won the
first try.

Act as a Bridge

Simon and Garfunkle once wrote a song, "Like
a bridge over troubled waters, I will lay me down." (It
has nothing to do with this section, but it's a great
song). A salesman or telemarketer should bridge the
gap between the company and the customer. A
customer provides input and criticism about your
products. He provides needs, wants, complaints.
Listen to them, and take them back to your
management. They form the basis of tomorrow's
products. Remember, the biggest sales started with a
complaint. For example, one of the big hamburger

chains started when a customer said, "Look at these lousy, no-good hamburgers."

Patience

Top salesmen no longer go for the quick sell. Selling should be based on truth, integrity, and sincerity. Always tell the customer what he wants to hear. Take the time out to send information first, then go for the sale. Always try to be helpful, providing service, and information that the customer needs or wants. Remember, the biggest accounts sometimes take months, or even a year or more to get. They take many phone calls, sending information several times, before a sale is made. There is a proverb, "What is the most beautiful word in any language? Yes. And what is the most useful? Patience."

Service

Service is supreme. Your service should surpass that of your competitors. For example, let's say you have a customer who lives in Athlete's Foot, Wyoming. After your customer places an order, call and check your order department to make sure that his order was shipped promptly. And if you're in the area, you might take a ride into Athlete's Foot.

Chapter 6: Attitude

Attitude

Their's a proverb, "Is the glass half empty, or half-full?" It's all how you look at it. A "positive attitude" is essential for all who sell or want to succeed at anything. Look at the "positive" side of things.

A true positive attitude doesn't mean just putting on a positive face, and ignoring your problems. It means <u>meeting</u> your <u>problems</u> with <u>faith</u> that you <u>can and will solve them</u>. Then, devoting your energy, not to complaining or worrying, but to positively <u>working</u> on your <u>problems</u>: <u>analyzing</u> the problem, <u>thinking</u>, <u>planning</u> solutions. Then, one by one, <u>following your plans</u> to <u>action</u> - until the problems are solved.

For example, Jim Schnell sells spray paint specifically designed for painting graffiti. He has a good line - paints designed for bathrooms, school buildings, bridges, subways, even the teacher's car. Then, one day there's a problem: A can of spray paint explodes in the customer's face. The customer is mad—navy blue mad . . . When the salesman comes home from work, he finds his house is spray painted with graffiti.

At first, Jim Schnell is upset. Then, he looks positively at the problem; Why, this is an opportunity. He realizes this is "free" advertising. He calls the customer and asks if he'd also spray paint his car. Under the graffiti on his house, and his car - he puts "American Graffiti Spray Paint Co.", To order call 241-1493 . . . He is soon flooded with orders.

Be Positive

Look for the "positive" side of things. Especially look for the positive side of your product. But also look for the positive side of the weather, the economy, or whatever else is going on. People like to be around, talk to, and buy from positive people much more than negative or cynical people.

Even be positive when the customer express an objection. First agree by saying "Yes . . . but . . . then express a positive part of the product that handles the objection." Or start answering objections with, "I'm glad you mentioned that . . . (Then, follow with an explanation of how the objection/problem is solved.)

For example, "That washing machine you ordered through the mail . . . It got stuck in the mailbox . . . Well, you needed a bigger mailbox anyways . . . It shrunk your shirt to the size of a mitten . . . Well, put in another shirt, and you'll have a pair of mittens."

Confidence

Always go in - confident that you're going to make a sale. A customer senses your confidence (or lack of), and will tend to fulfill your confidence (or lack of). You need to have utmost confidence in your product: that it is something your customers really want or need. So first, you must believe in what you are selling. Even if you know and believe in your product, and have a good sales line, if you don't have a good image of yourself, selling can be rough.

You need to have a good idea of yourself. An inner feeling that you will succeed. Some call it self-confidence. Here's a study of 2 salesman; 1 with and 1 without self-confidence. Consider Bill Harris, bright, young, sort-of-a-jerk salesman. Bill lacks self-confidence. After a tough sales call, Bill says, "Well, Billy boy, you're a real bonehead . . . You should have been able to sell that guy. That's 5 out of the last 6 you lost. Maybe you should give up selling. My mother always said I was a jerk. Or take John Shepard, a man who has real self-confidence. John says to himself, "Even though I lost 28 sales in a row, I feel like I'm almost there. With each sale I blew, I'm getting closer."

The point is John Shepard eventually made a sale.

Expect the Sale

If you go into a conversation - expecting the sale - the expectation will tend to be fulfilled. Likewise, if you go into it with the belief - I doubt I'm going to sell this customer - again, you expectation will likely be fulfilled - that of "not selling". One salesman was cold calling (really cold calling - from Alaska). He was selling leftover hotcakes from one of the big pancake houses. The hotcakes made good footwarmers. He was selling them to Eskimos who stuffed the pancakes in their boots.

Each time he called, the salesman expected a sale, Eskimos are a tough sell, and he usually had to accept payment in whale blubber or ice cubes. Once he called the Army, and tried to sell them pancake footwarmers. The army agreed if he could make the pancakes bullet-proof. He contacted the pancake house who said they had some old "rubbery" pancakes that had been sitting around for years. It worked, and he sold the rubbery pancakes for $10,000 a piece to the Army.

Hence, expect the sale, and you will have more sales.

Throughout the conversation, always assume you are going to make the sale. Then, when it's time to close, give the customer a choice, "Would you like to pay by check or mastercard?" . . . Or "Would you like 10 boxes of brass fittings or 20?" Or "Would you like a box mailed now, or in 30 days?"

Be Interested in People

If you're not interested in people, and if you're not interested in helping people, then you may be in the wrong field. If you're sincerely interested in people, in helping people, and in helping solve their problems, then you'll be successful in telemarketing. But to be interested in people, you've got to listen to them, ask about them, sympathize with them.

Here's a typical concerned salesman:

Salesman: How are you today?
Customer: I just lost $25,000 in the stock market.
Salesman: (thinking, "Oh, the poor moron") . . . Sorry to hear that, sir. How did it happen?
Customer: It happened right while I was drinking a cup of coffee. . . My investment went down the drain even faster than liquid plumber.

Enthusiasm

One of the most important things in selling, especially over the telephone, is <u>enthusiasm</u>. It should come across in your voice. You should be so filled with enthusiasm, that even when you sneeze - it's enthusiastic. The customer should think, "Gee, this guy really knows how to blow his nose." One of the keys to enthusiasm is to love your work. If you don't love your work, at least love your product. If you don't love your product, at least love your secretary . . . The idea is to find something about your job that you love.

The best salesmen are enthusiastic about their product and enthusiastic about life. Your enthusiasm will come across the phone lines and transfer to your customer. Let's say you're selling potato peelers. One might say they're just potato peelers. Only a potatohead would say that. A good salesman would say, "These potato peelers can peel a potato so thin, you can stretch one potato halfway around the world . . . And think of all the frequent flyer miles you can get . . . just from peeling potatoes."

Be "High-Energy"

"High-energy" people sell better . . . So how do you get the energy? Three main means of raising your energy level are by 1) taking vitamins, 2) exercise (on a regular basis - this doesn't include walking from the bedroom to the bathroom), and by 3) getting a good night's sleep.

A multiple vitamin/mineral supplement each day can help you perform at your peak. Remember, people need iron just like the steel industry needs iron. Actually, right now, the steel industry needs a miracle.

Exercise keeps you from becoming a fat blob . . . More importantly, it increases your blood flow, helps your heart, and also helps Vic Tanny. Whether you walk, run, ride a bike, or swing from trees like Tarzan and the Apes, exercise can help you feel better, and sell better.

Sleep recharges your body, so that when you wake up, you'll feel like an EverReady Alkaline Energizer. If you don't get enough sleep, or a good quality "restful" sleep, you'll go to work tired and sluggish.

Emotions

Better strong emotions than no emotions. Share the customers joy and sorrow. Better yet, if you can transfer some of your emotions, especially enthusiasm to your customer, the product is sold.

Get excited about what you are selling, and the customer is bound to get excited too. This especially applies to selling for charities. If you believe strongly in the charity, for example - fighting muscular dystrophy, or cancer, . . . the customer will believe in the cause too, and buy whatever junk you're selling.

For example, one salesman sold subatomic particles . . . He sold all different types: neutrons, protons, kaptons, gluons, mesons, and morons . . . One customer placed a big order for 3 zillion neutrons, and a bunch of Elmers gluons to hold them together . . . When the order arrived, the customer was upset because his assistant sneezed and lost it all.

The customer became very emotional—a combination of very upset, very angry, and very sore (after being bombarded by flying neutrons). The salesman countered with strong positive emotions: enthusiasm, confidence, and reassurance not to let one sneeze ruin his laboratory. The result: the salesman ended up not only selling more neutrons and Elmers gluons, but he also sold a neutron net, which he made out of some of his wife's hair

curlers. He took $3 worth of hair curlers and sold them for $100,000 to the laboratory.

Act Alive

Nobody wants to buy anything from a deadbeat. Put some life in your voice. If necessary, eat a dozen hot peppers. Have a friend drop some icecubes down your back. Do whatever it takes to perk you up.

One telemarketer was selling tickets to the local wrestling matches. He'd start off, "How would you like some tickets to the wrestling match? He had a very mediocre response. But when he found out about who was wrestling, the holds they were using, and the activities at the ring, he came alive. He'd state, "Do you know who's wrestling this week? Why, it's Captain Pork Chop. He'll be taking on the Mad Chicken and Carl the Cactushead. There'll be plenty of kicking, scratching, nose smashing, and heads bouncing on the mat. . . . You won't want to miss it."

Put a Smile in your Voice

Is there a smile in your voice? Or maybe there's some bubblegum in your hair? A smile is better. Somehow, it will come across. Smiles tell you something. When you see a person smiling, you wonder: he's either happy or stupid . . . Either way, people will like you for it.

Always Learning

The best in telemarketing, just like the best in any field are <u>always learning</u>. The more you learn about selling, the more you learn about your products, the more you learn about your customers, the more that you can <u>improve</u> your technique. Thus, the goal is to continually learn to continually improve.

There's a proverb, "You must always be growing - just like a toenail." Let's say, you're selling broken pieces of fine china . . . And you get a genuine teacup that Ronald Regan dropped on the floor . . . The old method was to sell all the broken pieces of the cup as a lot. But remember your toenails, which are always growing . . . In other words, you might try selling each of the broken pieces separately - to many customers. The same principle applies to land or anything else valuable. Hence, the success of the "timesharing" deals, where a piece of property is sold 52 times, 1 week per year, to 52 different owners.

Get Training

Training can come from several sources: reading books, listening to tapes, taking courses, attending seminars, and watching how other successful salesmen are doing it. IBM trains their salesmen an entire year before they make a single sale. And after that, they're constantly training. If you want to be good, really good, get some training. Learn from some of the people who've done it before. That's the difference between a man and a cockroach. Both make mistakes. But a man can read books, take courses, and learn from watching others, while a cockroach is busy eating crumbs off the kitchen floor.

Seek Advice

If you run into a rough spell (and we all do), seek the advice of your manager, or even a co-worker. Ask him to listen to you making a call or two. Then, ask "What am I doing wrong?" or, "How might I improve?" Even some of the best salesmen can use advice.

For example, let's say you are selling half burned-up furniture. (There was a fire at Harry's Furniture Store, and you have the opportunity to sell the half burned-up pieces real cheap). You start your call, "Sir, do you have any burned-up furniture in your home?" (Your manager tells you to put a little fire in your voice). You continue, "No, well, have we got a deal for you . . . Something like this comes once in a lifetime. You can get half a sofa, or two-thirds of a chair for only $10. Yep, you guessed it; we're having a fire sale . . . You're wondering, does the sofa smell like smoke? . . . Are you kidding? The sofa has lung cancer. (Your manager reminds you, "Be positive"). You continue, "But don't worry, you can bring the sofa back to the dealer every week for chemo-couch therapy."

Chapter 7: How to Handle Rejection

When you lose a sale, do you flush your head down the toilet? Some customers are extremely hard to sell. When you lose a sale, <u>learn from it</u>. Success comes often from experience. And experience comes mostly from your blunders. The difference between a successful person and a blockhead is: the successful person learns or tries to gain something from his mistakes or "no-sales", while a blockhead either gets depressed or learns nothing.

Losing a Sale

Whenever you lose a sale, look at it as an opportunity to learn. Remember, we learn the most from our mistakes, from lost sales. Also, as stated in another section, selling, like business and other areas of life, is all based on percentages. You may have to make 10 calls, or 15 calls just to get one sale. Advertisers of large corporations spend $25,000 up to 1 million dollars on a single ad, often hoping just to "sell 1 or 2 % of the listening audience.

One salesman sold used underwear. He thought he almost had a sale. Then, the customer asks, "What condition are they in?" The salesman answered, "We have 3 grades: Grade A, which is just slightly stained, Grade B, which has darker (or yellow) stains and only minor odor, and Grade C, which stinks like hell." For some reason, the customer decides not to buy. Then, after analyzing the loss, the salesman finds that he hasn't sold any Grade C underwear. He decides to just give a sales pitch on Grade A and

Grade B in the future. His sales go up. And he decides to give the Grade C underwear to a friend for Christmas.

Rejection

Don't ever take rejection personally. Remember, you don't buy everything you see or from everybody you talk to either. Very few people could afford to. So, you're going to get some rejections; it's part of life. Actually, don't look at it as rejection; it's probability. All salesman realize that they're only going to sell a <u>percentage</u> or part of the customers they call. It may be 1 out of 5, or 1 out of 10, or 1 out of 20, depending on what they are selling, and how good the economy is doing.

So, when you don't make a sale, you're just checking off the 1st, 2nd, 3rd, until you get to the 5th when you will make a sale. Hence, with every call you make, even if it's a "no", it increases the probability of success the next time.

One salesman sold guitar picks. And not the run of the mill guitar picks, he sold genuine guitar picks made out of monkey's toenails . . . He sold two types: "regular" and "Big Toe" guitar picks. Well, for some reason, nobody is buying monkey's toenails. 8, 9, 10 calls, finally on the 11th call, someone wants 5 "Big Toes". You see, it's all in the numbers; eventually, if you keep calling, it will pay off.

All salesmen, and nearly all people get rejected. The difference: successful people, and successful salesmen <u>persevere</u> and <u>learn from their mistakes</u>. For example, a friend of mine is a janitor, and a piece of gum got stuck to his shoe. The manager happened to come by. The gum had caused his right shoe to stick to the floor, so he tried mopping in a circle. When the manager asked him to mop the other side of the room, and he tried to lift his foot, the gum stretched from the floor to a couple feet in the air like a stringy rubber band. The manager fired him. But did he quit janitorizing? No. From that day on, he sprayed the bottom of his shoes with Teflon. Never again did a piece of gum stick to his shoe. Of course, he slipped and fell on his rearend a few times.

Don't be Afraid to Fail

Abe Lincoln said, "Courage is not the absence of fear; it is the conquest of it."

"Don't count the strokes, just keep swinging." The law of averages will pay off, and eventually you'll hit the ball. Would you believe that when Jack Nicholas was young, he took 77 strokes to hit the ball into the first cup . . . (so what if he was 3 years old). He was determined that no matter how many times he failed, no matter how many times his brother called him an uncoordinated klutz, he would keep hitting until he got the ball in. Can you imagine if he quit - golf would never be the same.

Guts

Guts and courage are important in making the initial call, and in asking for the sale. One technique for getting guts is by remembering someone or some phrases that make you feel courageous. Maybe it's an old western with John Wayne, or Arnold Schwartznegger in The Terminator, or Rocky Boxing, or an Olympic diver diving off a cliff or Michael

Jordan shooting a basketball, or Captain Kirk saying "Beam me up, Scotty".

You might remember something from earlier in life like your friend throwing you a touchdown pass, or you hitting a home run, or your friend stepping in some dog crap and tracking it all over his parent's house, then getting the brilliant idea of wiping the dog crap on his sister's shoe so it looked like she did it. . . . Or any other act of courage.

Quick Recovery from No-Sales

There's a Japanese proverb, "Fall down 7 times, get up 8." Everybody falls. The successful person is the one who keeps getting up. Don't dwell on lost sales, just keep plugging away, keep making those phone calls.

A Brick Wall

Every once in a while, you hit a brick wall. It's usually a customer. Maybe, it's a big account you just can't seem to sell. Maybe, it's several smaller accounts. Maybe you drove into a brick wall with your car.

In any case, it's good to remember a quote from Napoleon Hill, "With every adversity, there's a seed of equivalent benefit." Step back a little, and take another look at the brick wall. Maybe get up and get a drink of water. Try to truly understand why the customer won't buy, and what his problems really are. Maybe look at the wall, "one brick at a time". That is, break the problem down into its component parts. When you can take apart that key brick, the whole wall will come down.

Persistence: never give up. Even though you may smash 4 or 5 of your fingers, keep pounding away. Eventually you'll hit the nail in (or smash you 5th finger).

For example, one salesman was selling lumber, but customer after customer kept complaining, "The economy sucks . . . I can't afford to buy lumber to build" . . . The salesman was nervous; he was sweating like a pig. He even began to look like a pig.

He decided to take a break, and went outside. He stopped in a nearby 7-11 and bought an ice cream bar. Stuffing his face made him feel better. As he was finishing the ice cream bar, an idea hit him . . . "Why that's it. Ice cream sticks are made of wood." So, he started calling and selling wood to ice cream companies. Then, he sold popsickle sticks. He soon sold more wood than he had in 5 years before put together. Plus, he got to fulfill one of his dreams: he got a free ride in a Good Humor truck.

Chapter 8: Sales and Promotions

The Gimmick

Many great sales pitches, especially over the telephone, or the ones in the mail, have a gimmick. A gimmick is something different, or "extra" that you are giving in addition to the actual product. For example, a common gimmick is a "lifetime membership". Thus, once you pay X dollars, you'll be "saving" money the rest of your life. This gimmick is very successful when selling land or time-sharing, or vacation packages.

Another popular gimmick is "contests". If you buy our magazines, we'll enter you in our contest, and you'll have a chance (albeit only one in a zillion) to win some big prize, usually a car, a vacation, or money. One salesman used the gimmick that if the customer bought a big sale, he would personally fly out to the installation site to make sure all went well.

So, what's your gimmick? What's your "added incentive" for the customer to buy from you now?

Contests and Raffles

Contests can be very effective in getting people to send in cards, and also order. They are probably over-used, but are nevertheless still successful. In a typical contest, you offer 1 to 4 big prizes, such as a new car, a boat, an all-expense paid trip to DisneyWorld or Hawaii, etc. Then, you offer a prize that everybody else wins, such as a free "poptart", or a pack of "Wrigley's spearmint gum". The odds of winning one of the "big" prizes are 1 in 10 million, while the odds of winning the pack of chewing gum are very good.

Note: even the big prizes, your company should arrange to get "free" because you are "advertising" their product for them. The small or gimmick prize, your company should get a special deal on, preferably something that the manufacturer overproduced and wants to dump at a real low price.

Also, preferably people should have to call in to find out if they've won; that's when you give your sales pitch for the product you're trying to sell. And preferably, have the contest award the big prize from a drawing that is held <u>after</u> they order. (for example, if they call in July, the drawing is held the following September or October).

Give-aways

Give-aways are a good way of getting new customers, or getting more orders from existing customers. Good items (that people like) are tee-shirts (usually that say something) or customized with the person's name or initials. Also good are sporting equipment : golf balls, tennis balls, soccer balls, baseballs, bats, even a golf club or a tennis racket (for bigger orders). Also, popular are coffee mugs.

Bad give-away items are calendars (most people need one calendar and have about 50). Clocks and radios are also not good for the same reason. However, head sets for use in jogging may be good. Premium coffee or special herb tea may be good, but avoid that rotten moldy cheese from overseas. And never give away fruitcakes (unless your customers are fruitcakes).

Have a "Special" or "Sale"

"Sales", "Specials", "Reduced", and "Discounts" give a customer the idea that he is getting a deal. Many people are trained to shop for bargains, just like a squirrel is trained to gather nuts. Further, the sale or special should be for a "limited time" so the prospect has an incentive to buy now. Another popular incentive is to offer a "rebate". Nowadays, it's almost impossible to buy a car without getting a rebate.

Supermarkets use "sales" almost continually to bring people into the store and buy. I was shopping last week, when I saw a sign "Sale. 1/2 off - Rotten Bananas". I went to buy some, but they were all sold out. Human nature being what it is, more sales can be made if the customer thinks he's getting a "bargain", so don't be afraid to offer "sales", "discounts", and "specials".

Add a Bonus

To cinch the sale, it's a good idea to add a bonus . . . The bonus should relate to the customers "hot button". (hobby or interest) . . . For example, if he likes golf, send him some golf balls, if he likes tennis, send him some tennis balls, if he likes snow skiing, send him some snow balls.

Offer a Guarantee

Always give some sort of a guarantee. Even if it's only a guarantee that you'll ship the product within 30 days. Many department stores offer a "money-back guarantee", but what you're selling over the phone is often worthless, you may not want to offer a money-back guarantee. Instead, you may offer specific guarantees. For example, if you're selling those little red or green ties for garbage bags, offer your customers a free bag of garbage . . . And guarantee that the tie won't come apart—spilling garbage all over their front lawn—or you'll replace the garbage free.

A guarantee helps a customer to buy because it eliminates risk. You can tell your customer if he's hesitant: "There's no risk: the product is backed by a 30-day guarantee." The guarantee helps sell because it gives the customer peace of mind: (he doesn't have to worry if something goes wrong, your company will take care of it).

Preferably, offer a money-back guarantee. Most people loathe to take risks. By offering a money-back guarantee, you're eliminating their risk, which leads to many more sales. Even if you can't offer a money-back guarantee, at least offer some guarantee. For example, you guarantee to replace it if it fails at any time within 1 year. Or you guarantee, it will last 5 years or 50,000 miles. Or one company sold denture adhesive. They guaranteed that your teeth wouldn't fall out in the middle of a sentence.

Chapter 9: Overcoming Objections

Break a Case

A common objection is that the customer can't use or afford a full case now. Example:

Customer:	I can't order a 55-gallon drum now.
Salesman:	Let me put you on hold, and let me check with our plant manager . . . (wait a minute) . . . I talked to the plant manager and he owes me a favor, so he's willing to break the drum, and we'll give you just 20 gallons. And we'll still give you the same price per gallon, the same quantity, and the same discount as the 55 gallon drum. Doesn't that make sense to you, Joe?

A similar common objection is: Our stock is full right now and we don't need any more. Well, why don't you try 1/2 a case of our product and compare it to what you use now. The proof of the pudding is in the testing. That makes sense to you, doesn't it, Joe?

One salesman sold pig's tails. He sold "regular" and "honey-baked" pig's tails. He came across a person that didn't want one, so he offered to cut it in half for him and make a pigtail sandwich . . . The customer loved it so much he started a McPig franchise. He sold pigtail sandwiches, and he added a "lardburger" (made with 1/4 lb. of pure lard). Later, he noticed that a lot of tails were starting to rot, so he chopped them up and sold them as "nuggets".

Prepare Answers to Common Objections in Advance

Keep a list of answers to common objections nearby when you call customers. Also, review the list frequently until you're familiar with it. Some common objections are: the price is too expensive, I really don't need it, I already have one, I don't want any, and Not now, but maybe later.

Some solutions to "Not now" is to offer a <u>sale</u> (limited time), or <u>Introductory Offer</u>, <u>limited quantities</u> available, price will increase soon, or offer an <u>incentive</u> or <u>gift</u> for a limited time only. Objections are part of almost every sale. Don't let them get to you. Prepare for them. And look at them as "questions" that the prospect needs answers before he can buy.

One salesman sold high-speed cameras. Customers kept objecting that they made a "ticking" sound that was very annoying. So, the salesman suggested that whenever they load the camera with film, they stuff the camera with popcorn . . . Sure enough, fresh and even stale popcorn (like you buy in the great big bags for 99 cents) stopped the ticking. However, the salesman did warn customers not to use "cheese popcorn". Cheese dust tended to jam the camera.

Ask Questions

The best way to handle customer objections is to ask questions. Ask questions that lead the customer to discover the answer himself. This method, called the Socratic method because it was originated by Socrates, is highly effective in teaching and in selling.

It's usually good to <u>agree</u> with the customer even when he objects. You can do this by such phrases as "That's a good point." Or "I'm glad you mentioned that." Or "Yes, that's true, but . . . (then follow with leading questions . . .)

A typical customer objection is: I'll think it over.

Questions to ask: Why should you buy? What will you lose by not buying now? For example, Could you lose the special offer? The "sale" may be over tomorrow? Or Could the item be sold out?

For example, one salesman sold a custom line of jeans for heavy-set people called "Fatman" jeans. Customers kept objecting that they couldn't get into jeans, or worse yet, they couldn't get out of them . . . So, his company came out with a line of jeans for fat people. When customers typically complained about wearing jeans, the salesman would ask, "If someone asked you to haul ass, would you have to make 3 trips?" . . . He would then ask, "Would you like our 3-ass, our 7-ass, or our hippopotamus jeans?" By asking questions, meeting objections, and giving people a choice, more sales were made.

Overcoming Resistance

Often, when a salesman meets resistance from a customer, the salesman attempts to emphasize the qualities of the product. This is usually a mistake. It is better to emphasize "how the products fits into the person's life - how it solves a <u>particular need</u> of the person."

Give a Choice. One salesman sold special jeans for heavy-set people called "Fatman jeans". He gives the customer a choice: he can order a pair of 3-ass or 7-ass jeans.

Salesmen try to show off their knowledge of the product. It is better to seek to communicate, seek to understand your customer. When you better understand the customer, you can better help fill his particular needs.

Let's say, you're selling a product everybody needs: Cockroach Killer . . . However, you keep elaborating the benefits of your product, but are getting nowhere. Instead, stop advertising your product, and ask your customer, "So how do you kill your cockroaches?"

Customer:	"By stepping on them."
Salesman:	But they move pretty fast.
Customer:	Well, I'm a dancer.
Salesman:	Really, did you train at Fred Astair?
Customer:	Yes, I love to dance. I can do the waltz, the cha-cha, the mambo, the swing.
Salesman:	Maybe, you'd like an autographed picture of Fred Astair. Fred Astair himself used to buy our cockroach killer. It saved him a lot of wear and tear on his dancing shoes.
Customer:	Really . . . Well, maybe I'll try a half-dozen cans.

When the Customer Says "No"

There are two main methods of getting a customer to say "yes" after he has already said "No".

1. Lowering the price. If you keep lowering the price, you will eventually reach a point where the price equals the value of the product in the customer's

71

mind. When the price is below his perceived value, he is more likely to buy. Hence, many telemarketers don't offer their lowest price item up front. For example, they may first offer a $25 item (or ask $25 for charity), but if the customer says "No", they then offer a $15, or even a $10 item.

2. Increasing the value of the product to the customer. This is done mainly by explaining added benefits that the customer did not previously consider. Hence, it's best not to tell all the benefits up front. Save a few benefits in case the customer says No. The new information may lead to a new decision and result in a "sale".

3. Change the product to fit the times. Maybe your product seems old and outdated. When you describe your product, do you use words like "Elvis". Do you sell air freshener? It should not only sanitize the air, it should "Jordanize" the air (taking advantage of the current popularity of Michael Jordan).

When the customer says "No", don't try to "change his mind" . . . It's very difficult to get someone to admit they were wrong. Instead, try to tell him about some "valuable new benefit", some new features that will allow him to make a new decision. And hopefully, the new decision will be yes.

Sometimes, it takes 3, 4, 5, or more No's before you can get a yes. Remember, don't give up easy. Edison went through hundreds and hundreds of substances that didn't work before he found the right one to make a light bulb. Richard Nixon tried dozens of alibis and excuses to try to get out of the Watergate scandal until he hit upon the "phlebitis in his leg" trick.

The Customer Say's He Isn't Interested

Keep talking. Keep on with your sales pitch. Put more enthusiasm in your voice and emphasize the benefits to customer. The biggest sales are often made to customers who said they weren't interested . . . Determine what his objections are, then overcome them immediately. Then continue with your sales pitch; you don't want the objections to come up when you're trying to close.

One salesman was selling tickets to see the band, "The Boston Pot Bellies", . . . The customer said he wasn't interested. But then, when he described their music: "It's smooth like Boston Cream Pie . . . It's mellow like Jello . . . It sounds a little like Glen Miller if you're drunk and dizzy."

Hard of Hearing

Sometimes, when the customer says he's not interested, you need to suffer a temporary loss of hearing. Often, a customer says he's not interested when he really can't afford it, or he's busy, or he's having a rough day. The salesman should continue his sales pitch, hopefully trying to get the customer more interested.

For example, one salesman was selling memberships in "The Smiling Hogs Swim Club" . . . Of course, he started his sales pitch with, "How would you like to become a Smiling Hog?" Often they replied,

"I'm not interested." The salesman becomes "hard of hearing" and continues his pitch, "The Smiling Hogs are a happy group of men, women, and pigs all swimming in the same pool . . . "

Persistence

Perhaps the most valuable quality a person can have is persistence. Sheer determination. That was Edison's genius. It's also invaluable in sales. Some customers take longer to sell. You can't sell them the first time you call. They want to think it over, or they can't talk at the moment. Call back. Call back 2, 3, 5 times, or more if necessary.

Two brokers I know sold stocks. They each called the same customer. The customer said "No" to both brokers the first time. The one broker figured the customer wasn't interested and stopped calling. The other broker persisted, he called over 10 times, until finally 6 months later he made a sale - but the "sale" was for over $50,000 . . . Hence, it pays to be persistent . . . Or stated another way, you don't sell a million-dollar account the first time you call.

Another example is a salesman who sold "Do-it-yourself Divorce Kits" . . . The kits sold real well, and he had a lot of repeat customers. However, once in a while, he came across a happily married couple . . . But he didn't give up. He knew that sooner or later, they'd grow to hate each other . . . So he kept calling, and it usually paid off . . .

Find the "Real Reason"

J.P. Morgan once said, "A man generally does things for 2 reasons: One that sounds good, and the real reason." Analyze your customer's problems from his <u>point of view</u>. As Mark Twain said, "You've got to walk around in his shoes for a while (which is really hard if the customer has smaller feet than you do).

Once you've analyzed your customer's problems from his shoes, you can understand the "real reason" why he <u>will</u> or <u>he won't</u> buy. Then, discuss or show how you can <u>solve</u> the <u>real reason</u> in terms of <u>his</u> <u>wants, needs</u>, or desires. When the customer gives what you believe to be an excuse, like he's happy with his present products, you may ask him, "Yes, that's true, but is there any other reason?" Then, he may tell you the real reason.

Whatever reason or excuse he gives - <u>never</u> <u>argue</u> with him, and never counter with a statement that shows that the customer is <u>wrong</u>. When you prove the customer <u>wrong</u>, you put him on the defensive, and you almost always lose the sale. Rather than showing him to be wrong, seek to "solve" his reason, or <u>solve</u> his problem. For example, if he says he can't afford it, offer a reduced quantity, or a payment plan, or agree to hold his check 90 days, or accept deferred payment, or accept credit.

Once a solution has been found, state one final benefit of your product (or restate a previously mentioned benefit), and then quickly try to <u>close</u> the sale. Never linger on about a problem, once it is solved - move on.

For Hard-to-Catch Customers

If a customer is always on the run, going to a meeting, on his way to catch the plane, or he has to run and take a piss . . . Say "I'll tell you what . . . "If you're doing your job, you won't want to wait till you're down to the last lightbulb. You'll get a small quantity of our product, so you can <u>compare</u> our product to the competitors. The proof of the pudding is in the <u>testing</u>. Doesn't that make sense to you, Joe?" (Just remember to change the last couple words if the customer's name isn't Joe. Accidents do happen. I was talking to my mother, and I kept saying, "Doesn't that make sense to you, Joe?")

Solve the customer's problems. Here,
it is raining in the customer's living
room, so sell him an umbrella.

Chapter 10: The Closing

"Closing" Time

How long before you should try to close? . . . A
telemarketer can close a sale just as soon as he or she
has established the <u>real worth,</u> the <u>real benefits,</u> in the
<u>customer's</u> mind . . . If you try to close before that
time, you may appear like a high-pressure salesman
who isn't interested in the customer, and the customer
may become totally turned off.

However, you don't want to drone on and on
like a windbag or a Congressman. Remember, some
of the best speeches were short, such as The
Gettysburg Address or Hilton's speech on "what makes
a bellhop hop?"

For example, one salesman sold large 2 ft. in
diameter plastic earrings. (The company formerly sold
hool-a-hoops, but the company redesigned the hoops
and made them into large earrings.) The salesman
didn't want to close too soon, or the person would feel
like she was wearing two hool-a-hoops hanging from
her ears . . . The salesman had to establish that the
earrings were "stylish", "in", "hot", "elegant", and when
she walked into a party with the earrings, all eyes will
turn to her.

Getting the PO Number

After you've "made a sale", don't let the
customer off the hook until you get a purchase order
(PO) number. Customers might say, oh I've got
another call, I got to go, or I've got to get the PO, I'll

call you back. Say "Joe, do me a favor, I've got another line coming in here. Put me on <u>hold</u>, go <u>upstairs</u> and get the PO, and I'll hold on for you. Don't let him go; he might change his mind later.

Wrap Up

After the close, quickly summarize the order, what was bought, when it will be delivered, and how payment will be made. This avoids confusion later. Also, mention if any extra gifts or incentives will be sent. Then, finish with a "Thank you", and I hope you enjoy our 5 lb. bag of "Gourmet Bird Droppings". Good-bye.

Chapter 11: Selling to Tough Customers

Getting Past the Secretary

The Secretary always likes to have the Napoleon complex; she wants to think she's the decision maker. Always assume that you've talked to him (the customer) before. Never say, "Can I speak to the Plant Manager?" Say: "The Plant Manager, what's his name again? Secretary: Oh, Mr. Smith. Salesman: Yeah, Can I speak to him again?

Sometimes it helps to warm up the secretary. Complimenting her voice or ask her something about her home state - such as: how was the mud slide last week? Also, never make it sound like it's a "cold call". Say, "We've received a letter in the mail from your ---- - Department (but can't quite make out the name) requesting more information on our "Butter-fingers" lubricants. Make it sound like you're replying to a request made by them. (You're trying to help them).

Always assume you know who you're talking to. Assume that you've talked to him before. The plant manager, what's his name again? Assume the positive, that you'll get through. Otherwise, the secretary is the first one to not let you through.

When you Can't Get a Purchase Order Up Front, Offer a Free Trial

If you can't get money up front (a purchase order or credit card number), at least ask for the opportunity - to let the customer try your product at no risk. (If your products are good, most of the time, he'll end up buying them, and it may lead to repeat orders later).

For example, one salesman sold horses for breeding. One customer was a little ambivalent about buying horses over the phone, so the salesman sent the customer 2 females and one male for breeding on a 30-day free trial. The customer called back and said that the horses were healthy, but the male horse was gay . . . The customer was going to send back the horses, but the salesman convinced the customer to at least take the gay horse to a horse psychiatrist . . . The horse psychiatrist tried to talk the male into "at least going both ways" . . . The horse agreed so long as he was allowed to redecorate his apartment. Although the sale took a long while. (especially to decorate the apartment), the customer eventually PAID. Hence, offering a 10-day or 30-day free trial is often better than no sale at all.

Get the Customer to at Least "Try" the Product

Once the customer can touch and hold the product, he is <u>more likely</u> to <u>buy it</u>. So, even if you can't sell immediately, have a free 7-day, or 30-day free trial; go for it. For example, one salesman was selling perfumed diapers. He was meeting much resistance, until one lady called back and said she was surprised at how "soft" the diapers were. And that the perfume really smelled nice. In fact, she put some diapers around her house to use as air fresheners. So, he started giving a free trial. Sure enough, his sales tripled and everyone was sending him baby pictures. This led him to the idea of having a "beautiful baby" contest.

The Price

When a customer asks you the price? Or what is the cost? Don't just give a dollar figure. Always assume the positive. Thus you would reply, "That depends on how you buy it." . . . Then, give him a few choices, with each choice, assuming he will buy it. For example, if you are selling cookies, say, "If you pay in full, we can send you 2 boxes of cookies for only $100 . . . If you prefer, you can make payments, $12 per month for a year, and we'll send you 2 cookies each month. Of course, by the end of the year, most of the cookies will be stale." If the customer objects that the price is too high: then you need to show the big benefits of your product. You need to increase its value in the customer's eyes.

Give More for the Dollar

You've got to outsell your competition in price. You need to give your customers more for the dollar. "Give a customer more than he expects, and he'll be back." For example, you're selling grandfather clocks. Throw in an extra gift - like a free one-way ticket to Neptune. (which is something he wouldn't expect, and it's a lot further than your competitors, who are probably giving away tickets to close places, like Hawaii).

Also, beating the competition in price doesn't always mean having the lowest price; your product can also <u>last longer,</u> or require <u>less maintenance,</u> or <u>reduce downtime,</u> require <u>less repairs,</u> <u>save energy,</u> <u>save gas,</u> etc. Then, you can show your customer that your product <u>costs less to use per day,</u> or another comparison showing how your product has a lower "effective cost" because it lasts longer. This is like the famous Ivory Dishwashing liquid commercial that showed the "Ivory washed more dishes per penny" than the bargain brand.

Don't Just Sell Products, Sell Value

Anybody can sell eggs, but to sell a dozen Jumbo eggs for the same price as your competitors are selling Extra-large eggs; that's value. Or to sell something that will last twice as long for only 1.5 times the price; that's value. Or to go to a political rally, and the politician speaks twice as long; that's bullshit.

Chapter 12: Follow-up After the Sale

After the sale should <u>not be the end</u>, but the <u>beginning</u> of a long relationship with the customer.

Feedback

When was the last time you called up a customer you already sold just to find out how he's doing? Remember, even the best car salesmen rely on repeat customers and referrals. So at least every 1 to 3 months, call back customers you've already sold, see how they're doing, see how the product is performing, letting the customer know that you just wanted to make sure everything is going well. This builds trust and repeat business in the future.

The Aftersale

Always make sure to check that the customer is happy. This spreads good will and may lead to repeat orders. Even if he isn't happy, find out why, and rectify the situation. If there's a problem, forward the problem to Engineering, or Manufacturing, or your company President, or VP in charge of product development. Complaints are the key to new and better products.

For example, one salesman sold nuclear powered nasal spray. Two weeks after each sale, he called the customer. One customer complained that he squirted the nasal spray a little too hard and made a great big hole in his head . . . The salesman called in engineering, and they suggested using a great big cork to plug up the hole . . . The customer was grateful for the advice and the cork. Further, he recommended the firm to his friends or even to strangers who stopped and asked him why he had a cork in his head.

Saying Thank You

In the follow-up "After the sale" call, remember to say "thank you". Or send your customers a card or short letter "thanking them for their business". It creates good will and leads to repeat sales later.

Art Linkletter once interviewed a little boy, asking "What were the two most important words you mother taught you?" He replied, "Please" and "Thank you".

Courtesy Calls and Referrals

Perhaps the best source of new business is old business. About a week or two after your customer has received the merchandise or service, make a courtesy call to see if they are happy with it. Ask what they thought of it. Take notes - whether they are compliments or complaints. Then, ask for referrals. Ask if there is anyone else, a friend, relative, or associate who might be interested in your product. If the person doesn't want to give a referral, state that you won't mention who it was that gave the referral.

These referrals are the best source of new sales. It is much easier to sell a referral than a totally unknown customer. You can even mention some of the compliments about your product from the original customer (remember those notes you took).

One salesman sold camel-hair coats. A week after each sale, he called the customer. He asked, "And how do you like your camel-hair coat?" The customer replied, "It fits okay, but the coat has fleas." The salesman jotted down: Fits okay - has fleas . . . The salesman said, "You should have bought some flea and tick spray for your coat. But you're in luck, we're having a special on some right now." . . . "How many fleas does the coat have - 10 million, 100 million, or a billion?"

Customer: "At least a billion."

Salesman: "Then you'll need 100 cans of flea spray . . . And right now, if you buy 99 cans, you get 1 free." . . . "Oh, by the way, is there anyone you might recommend, friends, enemies, relatives, ex-wife, mother-in-law who might be interested in a camel-hair coat?"

Sure enough, the customer gave 4 referrals, out of which the salesman sold 2 more coats and 200 more cans of flea and tick spray.

In the long run, the salesmen who make the most money, make it from <u>referrals</u> and <u>repeat customers</u>. After the sale, wait a few weeks to make sure the customer has received the product, then call your customer and find out if everything is all right.

What customers really want is: courtesy and service. Give him more than he expects and he'll be back. Further, if you give him good service, he'll recommend you to his friends, relatives, and business associates. "Remember your customers, and they will remember you." "What goes around, comes around." Give good service, and follow-up after the sale, and next year, your old customers will be your easiest sales.

Follow-up after the sale. After the sale, most salesmen disappear, while a good salesman "licks his customer's shoes" (This is not advised for wood shoes—it causes splinters). In other words, he calls the customer to make sure everything is all right.

Increasing Sales from Existing and Previous Customers

Most salesmen spend most of their time trying to get new customers. However, it is far more profitable to get more business from <u>previous</u> customers. You can call on previous customers to order the <u>same product</u> again (nothing lasts forever). Depending on the product, the customer may order once a week, once a month, or even once a year.

You can also increase sales by getting previous customers to order <u>new</u> or other products, different from what they ordered before.

Studies have shown that it is much more difficult to get a totally new customer. Your company is a stranger to him, and he is usually content with sticking with his existing sources of supply. However, an existing customer of yours is already familiar with you and your company - so no hard sell is needed. He is more willing to listen to you about any specials, or new products available. That's why most businesses sell most of their products to <u>regular</u> customers. So don't forget your regular customers, that's the best place to increase your sales.

Reviving Inactive Customers

Many times customers drift away like a pair of sunglasses that you left at the beach. These customers are often picked up by other companies (just like your sunglasses are picked up by beach bums). Remember, it's ten times easier to revive inactive customers than it is to get new customers (although don't count on getting your sunglasses back from the beach bums).

The great majority of the customers leave because they're neglected. Just a simple call saying, "Hello, you are missed . . . We haven't heard from you

in a while, but we do appreciate your business . . . "
And most of the customers will order again. In some
cases, you may run into a complaint - which caused the
customer to stop buying. Apologize for the error, and
tell how your company already has or will rectify it . . .
Then, it's a good idea to offer some sort of "special" or
added incentive to get the customer to order again.

For example, one salesman sold 50 gallon drums
of Genuine Imitation Maple Syrup . . . He called one
inactive account, "Mary Lou's Flat-as-a-Tire Pancake
House" . . . On this occasion, he ran into a complaint.
"Mary Lou, there's no need to worry. This time, the
drum won't leak syrup all over your floor . . . I know
your floor is still sticky . . . I'm throwing in a free box
of Spic N' Span . . . The drums we use now are
stronger than ever - they're reinforced with one of the
hardest substances known to man: stale dinner rolls."

In essence, you're painting a picture in the
customer's mind: not only is the product better, but
the packaging (the drum) is better, and he is getting
an incentive (a box of Spic N' Span) to go along with
it.

Repeat Orders
Keep a good filing system - a Roll-a-dex with
your clients' business cards, and put his "hot button" on
it - eg. golf, tennis, etc. For example, Joe Brown calls.
The salesman quickly looks through his Roll-a-dex. It
says: "Joe Brown, hobby: toothpick tennis (instead of
using a tennis racket, they try to hit the tennis ball
with a toothpick). Because of the difficulty, most
players use 2 toothpicks."

The salesman says to the customer, "Joe, How's
it going? . . . Good . . . Joe, right now we're having our
50th Anniversary, so we're sending our best customers
a box of toothpicks."

Chapter 13: Telemarketing Tips

Sell the Time Before you Sell the Product

There's a proverb, "You can talk to almost anybody about almost anything if you say it at the right time and in the right way." Thus, its not just <u>what</u> you say, but <u>when</u> you say it. Is it a <u>good time</u> for the <u>customer</u>?

In the first 10 seconds of your call, ask the customer: "Is this a good time for you?" Or "Can I have a few minutes of your time to tell you about ----- (whatever you are selling)" . . . For example, "Can I have a couple minutes of your time to tell you about a new device that will save you money on office supplies?" . . . (Just state one general main benefit in the opening) . . . "If not now, when would be a good time call?" You need to first sell the customer on the importance of listening to you before you can sell your product. If he says yes, or starts asking questions, then begin telling about your product.

Remember, "Timing is everything" . . . One of the biggest complaints customers have about telemarketers is that they call at the wrong time . . . Is it a good time to give your sales pitch when the customer is in the middle of a fight with his wife? Or during the last 2 minutes of a close football game? The customer will be upset before you even start. So, give the customer the courtesy of asking "When is a good time for you?" And whenever that time is, that's when you call back. You'll vastly improve your selling percentage that way.

Do you talk too much? The more you talk, the more the customer will think it's BS...One salesman talked so much, it literally began to snow...The salesman was kind, though, every time he talked, he gave the customer a shovel.

Call the Customer When He's Ready to Buy

But how do you know when he's ready to buy? Ask him. Most companies, and even households, have cycles when they will run out of an item. And any good businessman knows when he will start getting low on supplies. So, ask him, when would be a good time to call to reorder supplies. Keep a record of his delivery dates, so you can tell about how long it takes him between orders.

Remember, each customer is different - so keep a card on file for each one. Then, mark the date to call on your calendar, or if you use a computer, the "tickler" can remind you. It is during the "pre-agreed upon" calls, when the customer is "ready to buy" that you should mention any sales, specials, close-outs, new products, etc. That is the time to <u>increase sales</u> from regular customers. At the right time, most customers will appreciate your mentioning any specials, sales, or discounts. Also, allow for "seasonal" factors. Call before busy times, such as Christmas, Easter, or maybe the summer months are busiest. Know your business and ask your customers.

Make it Easy for the Prospect to Buy

Offer easy payment terms, credit, and accept credit cards. One company even accepted Bazooka Joe bubblegum wrappers (Of course, it took 5 billion wrappers to buy anything). Also have convenient delivery - when it's <u>convenient</u> for the <u>customer</u>. If you have a store, where the customer must pick it up - have convenient hours - open evenings, or weekends.

Suggestion Selling

Many times, salesmen will call on established accounts, who already know that they want. You can increase your sales up to 100% by suggesting:

1. That they stock up for certain holidays, or peak season periods, such as July 4, Labor Day, Memorial Day, Thanksgiving, Christmas, Mother's Day, Father's Day, Uncle's Twin Brother's Barber's Day, Moron's Day, etc.

2. They order related items to what they normally do - to give their customers a choice. Let's say, you're selling spaghetti noodles; they might try the green noodles, or whole wheat noodles, or noodles that are shaped like the American Flag (for patriotic customers).

3. They order related equipment. You can either stock the equipment yourself, or make a deal with a manufacturer to sell their equipment and drop-ship for you. This is a great way to increase sales. For example, if you're selling noodles, you might carry display racks, hand trucks, knives to cut open the shipping boxes, etc. One salesman even sold life insurance on the noodles.

Eliminate Risk

People fear risk. If you offer some type of money-back guarantee, or 7-day free trial, you can allay the fears of many customers who are hesitant to buy.

One company sold special brushes that allow handicapped people to pick their toes . . . (Many handicapped dream of picking their toes). Even though you can help some handicapped reach his dream, he might fear that it won't work, and he's being swindled. By offering a money back guarantee, the company is eliminating their fears, and saying "We stand behind our "Stinkomatic Toe Picker".

Don't Tell; Persuade

Nobody likes being "told" what to do. So, instead of telling, you persuade, or "give advice". One of my favorite stories is the fable of the "Sun and the Wind". Each claimed to be stronger. Then, along came a man wearing a coat. Each bet that they could remove the coat from the man. First, the wind tried. He blew and blew. But as the cold wind blew, the man held on to his coat. Then, the wind blew harder and harder still. But the harder the wind blew, the more the man clung to his coat. Then, the sun tried. Slowly the sun heated up the earth. First, the man wiped his forehead. Then slowly, the sun continued to warm up the earth. The man soon took off his coat. And as the sun got warmer, the more the clothing the man took off. The moral is: "Persuasion is stronger than force".

Go the Extra Mile

There's a proverb, "I'd walk a mile for a Camel." The point is: go the extra mile for a customer. Go out of the way, to find a book he might be interested in. If he's planning a trip to France, get and send him a brochure on France, or a guide to French art, or a French dictionary, or some french fries.

A salesman had a customer who was a big fan of Tom Cruise. So the salesman sent the customer a heating pad with a picture of Tom Cruise's face on it. The woman adored the gift and became a steady customer for many years.

That Little Extra

To succeed, it takes that little extra effort (actually, a lot of extra effort). So what should you do, pick up a hammer and start pounding in nails? No. (unless your desk is falling apart). The key is to:

1. Study your competition. Learn everything you can about him (or them). Learn who they are, what they are selling, why they are buying, what tv shows they are watching. What do you have that he doesn't have? A successful football coach carefully studies his competition every week - before the game.
2. Study your customer. What are his needs? What does he really want?
3. Study the location of your customers. Get some geographical knowledge of where the customer is from.

Spending an extra 1/2 hour a day, or even an hour a week studying your competition, your customer, the location, and your sales pitch will drastically boost your sales.

Length

A typical sales pitch on the phone should be much shorter than in person. The pitch itself should be 3 to 4 minutes, and 500 words or <u>less</u>. The shorter the better. People are <u>busy</u>, so avoid long pitches. When you first prepare your pitch, it may be a little longer (it may even be 1,000 words or more). Then edit it down, focusing on the <u>main benefits</u> to your customer. Does it save them <u>time</u>, or <u>money</u>, or <u>last longer</u>. Keep editing, and distilling the pitch, honing it down to perfection.

One salesman sold "Welcome" mats knitted out of doghair. He sold all different types: colliehair, poodlehair, Irish setterhair, even sheepdoghair. It seemed like he should have a doghair mat for everyone. Believe it or not, some people weren't interested . . . He even told them that no matter what you step in, just wipe off your shoes on the doghair . . .

Sales were down; you might say, sales were "for the dogs". Then he got a clue. One customer told him that he had so much hot air he could fill up the Goodyear blimp . . . This was an indication that he was talking too much. He took the customer's advice; he talked less and sold more. He also bottled his hot breath and sold it to a restaurant as a bread warmer.

There's a proverb, "silent waters run deep." Customers will respect you for keeping it "short and sweet." Remember, the best ad campaigns are one or two lines . . . "Plop, plop, fizz, fizz, oh what a relief it

Sell the time before you sell the
product. First, ask if this is a good
time for you, if not, when?...When the
earth explodes?...How about next
Tuesday?...Call when it's convenient for
you customer. Babies crying, hurricanes,
and earthquakes tend to distract
customers.

is" . . . "Where's the beef?" Fill in your favorite; I'll bet it's short.

The Best Time to Call

That depends on your market - who you are trying to reach. If you are trying to reach businessmen and working women at the office: 8:00 to 12:00, and 1:00 to 5:00 are the typical. Businessmen often take a "business lunch", which lasts longer, so try calling them between 2:00 and 5:00 pm. If you are trying to reach them at home: try 6:00 to 10:00 Monday to Thursday, and 10:00 to 6:00 Saturday, and 10:00 am to 9:00 pm Sunday.

If you are tying to reach mothers who stay at home, try 8:00 am to 12:00 noon, and 7:00 pm to 10:00 pm (after dinner). Mothers usually go out during the afternoon, so it is best to reach them in the mornings or the evenings. If the elderly is your market, you can call 8:00 am to 8:00 pm. They're often home during the day, but don't call after 8:00 pm, because many of them go to bed early.

Whatever your market is, you might do a little study to check when the best times to call are. Executives who are in meetings all day - try calling around 4:30 to 5:00, when they go back to their desks. Contractors are usually at the job site all day, so try to reach them early in the morning: between 7:00 am to 8:00 am.

Please note to take into account the different time zones. The above times are the best times <u>for the customer</u>. There's a three hour difference for the West Coast, two hours for the Rockys, and one hour for the central time zone.

Look for "Green Lights"

Always look for green lights, or buying points, as in "I'm not happy with my present grease." This is a "green light" that he's looking for a new brand of grease. Or, "My present grease isn't working that well." You have to jot down notes. After he tells you all his problems, then you can start offering <u>solutions</u>. "I think we can solve your problem. We carry an extra-greasy grease. It's made from the greasy hair of rock stars who haven't showered for months."

Take Notes

Keep a pen and paper in hand when you are calling, to jot down any pertinent, or otherwise useful information. Notes about the person - might reveal his "hot button" which allows you to sell him later, or little favors that you can do to win a customer. Or notes may help you improve you sales technique in general.

Get information such as birthdays and anniversaries, and then call him back, or send him a card to wish a happy birthday or anniversary. It's a personal touch that puts you in a category as not only being a salesman, but his friend. It's that personal edge or plus that gets you the next sale.

Here's a salesman's notes for a typical customer: Likes to golf . . . likes warm weather . . . has a big red Irish Setter who just tore up the living room carpet . . . watches Bob Newhart . . . reads James Mitchner, Steven King, and Garfield . . . likes Garfield the best . . .

Note: each of these things gives clues about the person. They can be used for an immediate sale, or saved for later reference for a follow-up sales call, letter, or promotion. For example, you might send him some golf balls, information on vacations in warm climates, a book on dogs, an article on Bob Newhart, or a book by Mitchner, Steven King, or Garfield . . . Or send him Garfield's autograph on a bag of kitty litter.

So, during a conversation, <u>always</u> be jotting down <u>notes</u>. What are his "hot" buttons, what are the green lights, what are his needs, what is his background, where is he from, where he has traveled to, and so on.

How to Talk

I asked one top-notch salesman, "How should I talk on the telephone?" He replied, "With your mouth" . . . Hence, avoid talking with your hands . . . the customer can't see it. More importantly: <u>emphasize</u> your words. <u>Increase your volume</u> on key words. And after you state an important point, <u>pause</u> . . . "This policy will pay you $1,000 a month after you retire, or will pay your heirs $500,000 after you croak" . . .

Also, vary the <u>pitch</u> in your voice - avoid a monotone. And if possible, vary the speed at which you talk so that it nearly matches your customer. In other words, don't talk at 90 miles-an-hour if your customer talks like a snail . . . However, if your customer talks with a stutter don't stutter too . . . This may upset him. It's best to talk at a rate you feel comfortable with, but is easy for your customer to follow.

Your Voice

What you say to a customer is very important, but equally important is <u>how you say it</u>. Think back to some of your best and worst teachers in school. Your best teachers were probably <u>vibrant,</u> <u>enthusiastic</u> speakers. Your worst teachers were probably <u>dull</u> and <u>monotonous.</u>

You don't have to sound like Barbra Streisand, but you should sound alert and self-confident. (A good example of a successful and self-confident individual is Bugs Bunny) . . . You don't want to sound weak or subservient. And you don't want to sound monotonous - so practice varying the pitch in your voice. Get some coaching from a friend or co-worker. He'll tell you some of your weaknesses.

So put some life and vigor in your voice. Also, every 15 to 20 minutes, get up and stretch or walk around, get a drink of water, clear your throat, otherwise, your blood won't circulate well and you'll sound stale (or it will sound like cobwebs are growing in your head). Maybe play some music in the background so it's not monotonous.

Returned Goods

If the customer insists on returning the goods with a nasty note, you could:

1. Call and apologize.
2. Have gravel dumped on his driveway.
3. Have pizza delivered to his house every hour.

A better solution is to emphasize to your customer that instead of sending the product back that you'll extend the pay period. For example, you'll give him an extra 30 days. This avoids the expense of returned goods and the cost of freight. And it gives the customer the impression that you want to work with him, and that you're not just another high-pressure salesman.

Monotony and Boredom

Telemarketing by its nature is a repetitive task. Some people are not bothered by this. In other cases, the repetition can lead to monotony and boredom. If boredom sets it, sales can drop. To avoid boredom, you might vary your pitch a little. Or better yet, <u>listen</u> more. Ask questions about the people. People are fascinating, especially if you get to tell about their adventures.

A salesman was getting into a rut. In fact, he was sitting in a hole in the floor. Then, he started listening to one woman who was traveling in Egypt. In the Sahara desert, she lost her wedding ring (which she found out later that her husband got from a box of Cracker Jacks). She began searching for her ring, but all she could see was sand and people with towels over their head. She dug in the sand for hours, finding only cactus roots and camel turds.

Vary Your Routine

It's easy to get into a rut. Vary your daily routine. Get up at different times. Eat something different for breakfast. Read a new book. Try something different for lunch; instead of a Big Mac, try Chicken McNuggets. Or go to a different restaurant entirely. Or stop and see a new site at lunch, or after work - go to new places, see new faces. And it doesn't necessarily cost much. There are thousands of book and tapes you can rent for free at the library.

Variety is the spice of life. It also leads to new ideas. And new ideas lead to growth. Mike Rivers tried the variety technique. He got so many ideas, and was growing so wildly that his co-workers had to spray weed killer on him.

When Necessary Push Yourself to "Start"

Sometimes procrastination creeps in. When it does, look at your "To Do" list. Suppose you've set a goal of making 10 calls per hour. So every 5 minutes, push yourself to start dialing, and just "jump into" the sale. There's no time like the present, so just keep diving in.

A friend of mine spent his honeymoon by going up to a beautiful lake in Canada. His wife was the type that wanted to tiptoe into the water. My friend wanted to prove his masculinity, so he just dove right in. Of course, he froze his ass off . . . The water felt like it was left over from the ice age. But that's how you learn. Nobody learns by just sitting along the sidelines and watching a baseball game. You've got to come up to bat. And you're not going to hit a home run with the bat sitting on your shoulders. You've got to <u>swing</u> to hit the ball.

Chapter 14: Preparation Before the Call

Planning and Organization

Take some time each day, and each week for planning. Plan what you are going to say, how you will respond to questions. Plan who you will call. Plan, organize, and prioritize. Ben Franklin said, "Let all things have their places, let each part of your business have it's time." Can you imagine building a 100-story building without a plan? Any large goal, requires considerable planning. Even the President's barber gives the President a blueprint of how he's going to cut his hair.

Goals and "To Do" Lists

The top people in any field have <u>goals</u>. To help them achieve their goals, they break down the goals into a series of steps. These steps are broken down by year, month, by week, and by day on "To Do" lists. The "To Do" lists give the individual tasks they need to do to reach their goals. Using "To Do" lists is a practical means of reaching a worthwhile goal.

One salesman sold a line of sweaters that were hand-knitted out of cigarette butts . . . The sweaters never needed ironing; the customer just threw the sweater on the floor and stepped on it. The salesman was doing fairly well selling the sweaters to smokers and people who hung around bowling alleys.

Then, one day an idea hit him. Why not make a "smoking jacket" out of cigarette butts. He wrote down the idea on his "To Do" list. Then, with the help of his wife, he made a sample smoking jacket by gluing a bunch of cigarette butts to the outside of his suit coat.

He wore the smoking jacket to a meeting with the company president . . . The president liked the idea, and gave the salesman a promotion, a raise, and a free pack of cigarettes. Hence, having goals and using "To Do" lists pays off.

Set a Goal and Go For It

Think of something you really want; maybe you'd like a new car, or a new house, or a new wife. Any sharpshooter has got to have a target to aim at if he ever is going to become good. (Although in most states, it's against the law to aim at your wife). Emerson said, "Men hit only what they aim at. Therefore, though you may fail immediately you had better aim at something high."

Give yourself a challenge. For example, I dare you to sell 500 cases in one week. "Dare to dream, and what you dare to dream, dare to do." There's a proverb, "Kiss enough frogs, and you might find a prince". (But more likely you'll get warts.)

Bonuses

First, set a goal and go for it. Then, reward yourself and your employees when you reach that goal. Bonuses should be frequent - not annually. Thus, give a bonus every week, or at least every month that your salesmen reach their goals.

For example, one salesman sold fine clothing. What's more, the product was good for the environment (the clothes were "recycled"; they were originally old smelly dish rags). His goal was to sell 50 dresses per week and 2 wedding gowns (wedding gowns were made from premium smelly dishrags, used handkerchiefs, and old paper towels). Whenever he reached his goal - he gave himself a bonus. In general, the bonus should be significant—at least 5 to 10% of your commissions. Thus, if you earn $3,000 in commissions, the bonus should be at least $150 to $300.

Listen to Your Sales Pitch on a Tape Recorder

Make a taperecording of yourself. What do you sound like? A robin or a buzzard? Does it sound the way you want your customers to hear you? Would you buy from someone who sounds like you? (Heck no).

Practice working on your voice: the tone, how and which words you emphasize, your loudness, and your pitch.

- Are you too loud—do walls fall down when you talk?
- Are you too soft—do people say "could you repeat that"?
- Are you emphasizing the right words?
- Do you sound too nasal—well, blow your nose . . . Or get some nuclear-powered nasal spray.

In telephone sales, your voice is all important. Keep practicing, and honing down your presentation so that it sounds just the way you want it.

Motivation

Some people are highly self-motivated. Something deep inside them urges them on. Others are motivated externally: by a boss, a teacher, a parent, or a friend.

One key to becoming motivated is to have a pot of gold at the end of the rainbow. In other words, have some realistic goal to work for. It might be a new car, or a nicer home. Then translate this goal into how much you need to sell. But don't make it so big that you can't reach it. Make it something within your reach. Then, with each sale, with each day, you chalk up how you're getting closer to that goal.

Example: John Hansen sold balloons. He was having a hard time selling balloons over the phone to people who couldn't see them. Then, he wrote down his goal - to buy a new litter box for his cat . . . (his cat had an old litter box, so she was always peeing on the floor). Once John had a goal to work for, he started talking better, and thinking better. Then he got an idea. To attract the customer's attention, he started popping the balloons while he was on the telephone. One man almost had a heart attack. But the people started buying.

Where to Get Names of Qualified Prospects

If you sell technical or specialized products, your company might <u>advertize</u> in an <u>appropriate</u> magazine, or send out coupons, or advertizing cards in deck of cards with other companies, either to the local area, or nationwide. These ads or cards, when returned, represent leads or prospects. A good salesman should review the ads and cards, and if possible, make suggestions for improvements. The better the ads, and ad cards, the more and better prospects you will receive.

Other sources of prospects include:

1. The telephone book - both white and yellow pages.
2. Lists from trade associations and professional societies.
3. Lists of registered voters.
4. Lists of automobile owners.
5. Lists of business from your local chamber of commerce.
6. Directories that can be found in your library, such as Standard & Poors, the Thomas Register of manufacturers, Dun & Bradstreet, Moody's, etc.
7. Specialized lists that can be purchased from a "list broker".

Select Your Prospects Carefully

One of the first ways to increase your percentage of sales, and reduce wasted time is to carefully select your prospective customers. First, decide what type of individuals or companies could best use your product or service. Anybody might be able to use it, but who is most likely to buy. You can even go over lists of previous sales records to see who are most of your customers. Are they middle-aged men? Or young mothers, or bachelors, or the elderly. A little analysis can double or triple your sales in the future.

Second, obtain a list of qualified prospects (see section on where to get qualified prospects). Third, go through the list, and <u>weed out</u> undesirable or unqualified prospects, either by <u>size</u> (let's say you're looking for business with over 200 employees, or you're looking for men over 3 feet tall - weed out the shrimps) . . . Or maybe <u>location</u> - maybe you're only interested in the suburbs, or maybe your product sells best in the slums.

Exchanging Leads

Herein lies one of the keys to expanding and increasing your sales. Think of a <u>non-competitive telemarketing</u> company, or other company with which you can exchange leads.

For example, one salesman sold typewriters, he found that many of his customers also needed desks and chairs - so he exchanged leads with a relative who was an interior decorator . . . Think about it, do you have any friends or relatives who you can exchange leads with. Another good technique is to skim through the <u>index</u> of the Yellow pages - do you see any types of companies that you might be able to exchange leads with?

For example, one telemarketer sold lard over the phone. Naturally, his phone cord was greasy. Then, one day, he happened to meet a guy in a bar who seemed like a real potatohead . . . As luck would have it, sure enough, the guy sold potatoes. The "lard man" and "potatohead" started talking . . . Then, they exchanged leads (you need grease to make potatoes into french fries).

Qualify Your Leads

In the first 30 to 60 seconds, qualify your leads to make sure who you are talking to someone who <u>can</u> purchase your product. This avoids wasting time on unqualified prospects, and can double your productivity - i.e. double your sales.

For example, "I'm looking for the person in charge of maintenance, are you the person that purchases the maintenance supplies for your company?"

Or, if you are selling storm doors or windows, make sure the prospect is a homeowner. If you are selling memberships to a single's club, make sure the prospect is single. If you are selling a new type of eyeglasses, make sure your prospect has eyeballs.

Know Your Customer and
The Geographic Area He is From

Know a little information about the customer, and some background on the geographic area. Do a little <u>research</u> before your call.

For example, check into how the local football team, (college or pro) is doing, and any good hunting, fishing, golf, or other sporting events that are nearby. Maybe he lives in Orlando, FL (near DisneyWorld), or in Washington, DC (near the Smithsonian), or in Open Sewer, WY (near an open sewer). A little background knowledge makes for a good conversation.

In summary, all these steps listed can help you become a more effective and successful telemarketing sales person, and maybe even with a sense of humor (you'll need it).

Give The Gift of Laughter:

Humor Books

Also available from Humor Books:

The Secretary's Survival Guide: Offers solutions to problems facing secretaries every day. How to arrange meetings, travel, how to deal with difficult customers, and what to do when you run out of coffee. It also covers topics of job advancement, sexual harassment, and how to deal with malfunctioning equipment or malfunctioning co-workers. Makes a great gift.

The Cat Owner's Survival Guide: How can you tell a cat owner? all the little claw marks on their back...Or by the cathair that sticks to their suit...A fun book with some good advice too. Get it for yourself, a friend or a relative with cats. They'll need it.

The Dog Owner's Survival Guide: Do you walk around in chewed up houseslippers? Is your backyard a minefield of dogturds? Dog owners, this book is for you.

The Will to Live: the battle of a young boy against muscular dystrophy: A touching story which may cause you to both laugh and cry. Recommended for a friend or relative of someone with a debilitating illness. It is a book of hope.

Special: Buy 3 books, Get 1 free. Dealer inquiries welcome.

Order coupon	Price each	Qty.	Total
The Secretary's Survival Guide	9.95	____	____
The Cat Owner's Survival Guide	9.95	____	____
The Dog Owner's Survival Guide	9.95	____	____
The Will to Live	9.95	____	____
Effective Telemarketing	9.95	____	____

Subtotal ____
Postage (please add $1 per book) ____

Return this form with check
or money order to: Total: _____

Humor Books   Your Name_____
58 Donovan Place   Adress_____
Alexandria, VA 22306 City_____
(703) 360-5916   State_____Zip_____

Give The Gift of Laughter:

Humor Books